Spellbound
Beaded Tassels

A Spellbound Bead Co Book
Copyright © Spellbound Bead Co Publishing 2012

First Published in the UK 2012

Printed in the UK by Charisma Design and Print
for the Spellbound Bead Co

ISBN - 978-0-9565030-4-6   01494

Editor: Jean Hall
Pattern Testing and Sample Production: Edna Kedge, Pat Ashford and Victoria Pritchard
Photography: Spellbound Bead Co

Visit our website at www.spellboundbead.co.uk

Spellbound Bead Co
47 Tamworth Street
Lichfield
Staffordshire
WS13 6JW
England

Call 01543 417650 for direct sales
or your local wholesale distributor

Acknowledgements

A special thank you to everyone who has contributed to this book - those who have tested, proofed and made cups of tea; taken photographs, revived whirring computers and counted beads.

Also a big thank you to all of our customers who have bought kits, given us feedback and been very enthusiastic to see another Spellbound book. We hope that you enjoy the book and are planning to make tassels for everything.

Contents

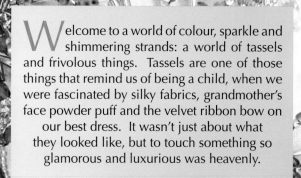

Welcome to a world of colour, sparkle and shimmering strands: a world of tassels and frivolous things. Tassels are one of those things that remind us of being a child, when we were fascinated by silky fabrics, grandmother's face powder puff and the velvet ribbon bow on our best dress. It wasn't just about what they looked like, but to touch something so glamorous and luxurious was heavenly.

This is a collection of beaded tassel projects from the last twelve years together with ten new tassel designs and many more inspirational projects for you to bead.

Each chapter starts with a main project which introduces the theme and takes you step-by-step through the construction of the headline tassel. Some of the chapters then lead on to more elaborate Inspirations projects and others to simple ideas that you can develop further.

The more complicated Inspirations projects are set out with step-by-step instructions, but it would be good practice to work through the first project in the chapter first. You will find that the Inspirations instructions refer to the first project in the chapter for basic techniques and to illustrate the order of work. The Inspirations all use the same basic tools as the headline project.

All of the main projects are graded for difficulty. Count the number of swirls underneath the title piece and compare them to the grading list below. If you want a really easy project to get started, try out the basic tassel instructions on pages 12 & 13, although you do have to choose your own bead selection for that one - what more excuse do you need for a bead-buying trip?

Choose a Project to Suit Your Beading Experience

Two Stars - simple techniques repeated several times to build up the design.

Three Stars - getting a little more complex but manageable for a beginner with patience.

Four Stars - several stages building on top of one another. Each stage is straightforward, but there are more of them to follow or there may be several thread ends to manage.

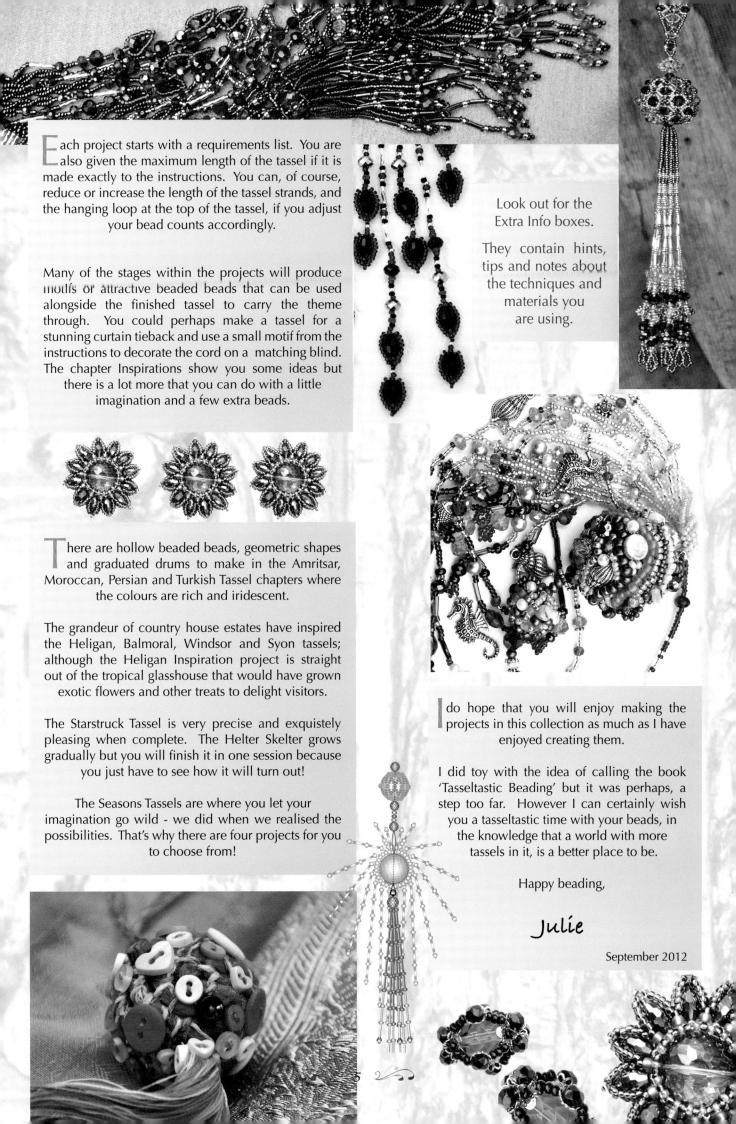

Each project starts with a requirements list. You are also given the maximum length of the tassel if it is made exactly to the instructions. You can, of course, reduce or increase the length of the tassel strands, and the hanging loop at the top of the tassel, if you adjust your bead counts accordingly.

Many of the stages within the projects will produce motifs or attractive beaded beads that can be used alongside the finished tassel to carry the theme through. You could perhaps make a tassel for a stunning curtain tieback and use a small motif from the instructions to decorate the cord on a matching blind. The chapter Inspirations show you some ideas but there is a lot more that you can do with a little imagination and a few extra beads.

Look out for the Extra Info boxes.

They contain hints, tips and notes about the techniques and materials you are using.

There are hollow beaded beads, geometric shapes and graduated drums to make in the Amritsar, Moroccan, Persian and Turkish Tassel chapters where the colours are rich and iridescent.

The grandeur of country house estates have inspired the Heligan, Balmoral, Windsor and Syon tassels; although the Heligan Inspiration project is straight out of the tropical glasshouse that would have grown exotic flowers and other treats to delight visitors.

The Starstruck Tassel is very precise and exquisitely pleasing when complete. The Helter Skelter grows gradually but you will finish it in one session because you just have to see how it will turn out!

The Seasons Tassels are where you let your imagination go wild - we did when we realised the possibilities. That's why there are four projects for you to choose from!

I do hope that you will enjoy making the projects in this collection as much as I have enjoyed creating them.

I did toy with the idea of calling the book 'Tasseltastic Beading' but it was perhaps, a step too far. However I can certainly wish you a tasseltastic time with your beads, in the knowledge that a world with more tassels in it, is a better place to be.

Happy beading,

Julie

September 2012

Essential Ingredients

Tassels can be made from many different materials and when it comes to beads you can be overwhelmed with the choices available. Most beaded tassels are made from a combination of seed beads, a few heavier weight beads to go at the ends of the strands and a larger bead to bring the top of the strands together. This quick guide will give you an introduction to these basic supplies and the extra items you might need for some of the patterns.

Bugle Beads

Bugles are small glass tubes which are available in several lengths. These projects use size 5 bugle beads which are about 11mm long, size 3 bugles which are about 6mm long & size 2 bugles which are about 4mm long.

Bugle beads can be a little rough or sharp at the ends - discard any misshapen or chipped beads as they will not lie properly and may cut into the thread.

Seed Beads

These are the small glass beads used for stringing tassels and fringes and for weaving intricate designs. They are available in many sizes and a myriad of colours and finishes.

The size of the seed bead is denoted as 11/0, 10/0, 9/0 etc - the larger the number, the smaller the bead will be. This book uses mainly sizes 10/0, 8/0 and 6/0.

Seed beads are manufactured in the Czech Republic or Japan. Czech seeds tend to be a more rounded shape than the Japanese seed beads and make slightly more flexible tassel strands. Most of the designs in the book are made with Czech seed beads.

Crystal Beads

Precision cut from very high quality lead crystal glass these faceted beads give a maximum amount of sparkle.

They are available in many shapes and sizes - this book uses rounds, rondelles & cross-hole drops.

Fire Polished Faceted Glass

To make a fire polished facet you must first make a round glass bead. Faceted faces are then ground away, one at a time, from the surface of the glass before the beads are placed in a kiln to 'fire polish'. The heat of the kiln is just hot enough to glaze the beads over into a glossy shine.

Tassel Top Bead

This is the large bead that sits at the top of the tassel strands. You can create your own decorated bead - see the Balmoral and Seasons Tassels or you can use a gorgeous feature bead. Make sure the bead you choose has a large enough hole to take multiple thread passes.
Plain wooden beads act as a neutral base for woven beaded coverings and bead embroidery.

Knitted Tubular Wire

Knitted from 0.1mm wire this material is flexible, surprisingly strong and very versatile. Supplied flat-packed or on spools, it is available in a choice of widths and many colours. You will need 15mm diameter tubing for the Seasons Tassels.

Jump Rings are the connecting links used in all sorts of jewellery designs. In tassel making they are used at the top of the tassel stranding. You can substitute the jump rings with split rings if you wish. Split rings are made from a double layer of wire so the thread will be less likely to slip through the gap.

Filigree Bead Cups

cup around the end of a bead to provide a filigree flourish to the design. They are also used for surface embellishment in this book. Available in many diameters and metal finishes.

Delica Beads

These are tiny cylinder-shaped glass beads used for accurate weaving as they will sit close together like bricks in a wall. They are available in several sizes and hundreds of colours. This book uses only size 11/0 Delicas.

Findings

You will need just a few simple findings to complete some of the tassel projects - there are some additional items you may need if you want to make the Inspirations projects as well.

Ribbon Ends are flat box-ends with serrated teeth to grip onto the end of a ribbon. Available in several widths you will need flat-faced pliers to close them securely.

Earfittings are used in a two of the Inspirations projects although there are many more possibilities for earring designs within the book.

Beading Thread

Sold under many brand names such as Nymo and Superlon, beading thread is available in several thicknesses and many colours. These projects all use a size D thread.

Stranded Beading Wire

Supplied under many trade names this is a very strong, flexible threading wire suitable for heavy beads or where a lot of wear and tear is to be expected. Different diameter wires with different flexibilities are available: a 7-stranded core is suitable for most of these projects. Always secure with French crimps and trim with wire cutters not scissors.

French Crimps are tiny metal cylinders that are squashed flat to secure stranded beading wire.

Threading Necessities

Beading Needles

Beading needles have a very slim eye so they can pass through a bead with a small hole.
Size 10 Beading is a general beading needle that is suitable for most of the projects.
Size 13 Beading is a little finer for multiple passes of the thread through the bead holes.

Sharp Scissors to trim the threads close are essential.

A Thread Conditioner such as Thread Heaven helps to smooth the kinks in the thread if you get into a knot or tangle.

A Fleece Bead Mat with a slight pile will stop the beads from rolling around and make it easy to pick up small beads with the point of the needle.

Clear Nail Polish is sometimes used to stiffen selected areas of stitched beadwork so that the desired shape is retained more firmly.

Pliers

You will need pliers for the projects using wire & findings.

Flat-Faced Pliers for gripping, opening jump rings & securing French crimps although you may prefer crimping pliers for this job.
Wire Cutters for trimming stranded beading wire, headpins and other rigid wires to length.
Round-Nosed Pliers for turning loops.

Tips & Techniques

There are a few basic techniques that you will need to work through the projects in the book. If you need a special technique for a particular project it will be explained within that chapter but for the techniques that apply to most of the designs this is what you need to read.

Using a Keeper Bead

Before you start a piece of beadwork you will need to put a stopper at the end of the thread. The easiest stopper to use is a keeper bead. A keeper bead is a spare bead, ideally of a different colour to the work, that is held on a temporary knot close to the end of the thread. Once the beading is completed the keeper bead is removed. That end of the thread is then knotted securely and finished neatly within the bead-work pattern.

fig 1

To Add a Keeper Bead - Position the keeper bead 15cm from the end of the thread (unless instructed otherwise) and tie a simple overhand knot about the bead (fig 1). When you thread on the first beads of the pattern push them right up to the keeper bead - this tension in the thread will prevent the keeper bead from slipping.

When the work is complete untie the knot and remove the keeper bead. Attach the needle to this end of the thread and secure.

Correcting a Mistake

If you make a mistake whilst you are following a pattern remove the needle and pull the thread back until you have undone the work sufficiently. Do not turn the needle and try to pass it back through the holes in the beads - the needle tip will certainly catch another thread inside the beads and make a filamentous knot that is almost impossible to undo successfully.

Protecting the Thread

You will be using a jump ring at the top of some of the tassels. When the tassel is complete and the thread ends secured and neatened, use a tiny dab of clear nail polish to seal over the thread as it passes through this jump ring. This will help to protect the thread and it should prevent the thread from slipping through the gap in the ring.

Finishing off a Thread End

You will need to finish off thread ends neatly and securely.

There are different techniques for finishing a thread whilst making a simple tassel and within a section of beadweaving.

Method for a Simple Tassel

The thread ends are always finished off above the tassel top or head bead (see page 11). Do not make a knot between the beads of a tassel strand as it will affect the overall flexibility of the strand.

Pass the needle through the tassel top or head bead at the completion of the last tassel strand. If you are making a simple tassel with a jump ring at the top there will be a tail of thread already there from the knot at the start of the work.

Make an overhand knot (fig 2) between the tail thread and the needle thread pulling the knot down tightly to the top of the head bead.

Repeat the knot and pass both thread ends down through the head bead to neaten before trimming as close as possible to the work.

fig 2

If you are making a tassel with a beaded loop, or a more complicated combination of beads above the head bead, you will need to finish off the thread end between those beads. Follow the instructions below for finishing a thread end within a section of beadweaving.

Method for Beadweaving

Pass the needle through a few beads of the pattern. At that position pick up the thread between the beads with the point of the needle. Pull the needle through to leave a loop of thread 2cm in diameter. Pass the needle through the loop twice (fig 3) and gently pull down to form a double knot between the beads.

fig 3

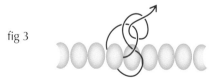

Pass the needle through five or six beads of the pattern and repeat the double knot. Pass the needle through five or six more beads before trimming the thread end as close as possible to the work.

Starting a New Thread

Occasionally you will need to add a new thread to the work. There are different techniques for adding a new thread whilst making tassel strands and for adding a new thread within a section of general beadweaving.

Method for a Tassel

A new thread is always joined to a tassel above the tassel top or head bead (see page 11). The thread is not joined or knotted within a tassel strand as it will spoil the overall flexibility of that strand when compared to the other strands of the design. In addition, the tassel top or head bead normally has a larger hole than the other beads in the design, so it is ideal for concealing the thread ends.

Work the tassel stranding until the thread length is insufficient to make the next strand of the design.

Make sure that the needle is emerging from the head bead and remove the needle from the thread end. Leave the thread end hanging loose.

Prepare the needle with a new thread length.

If the needle is being turned through a jump ring above the head bead you can simply tie the end of the new thread onto the jump ring (leaving a tail of 15cm) and pass through the head bead ready to make the next strand.

If you are working a tassel with a loop of beads, or a further bead sequence above the head bead you will need to tie a keeper bead 15cm from the end of the new thread.

Pass the needle through the head bead ready to start the next strand (fig 4).

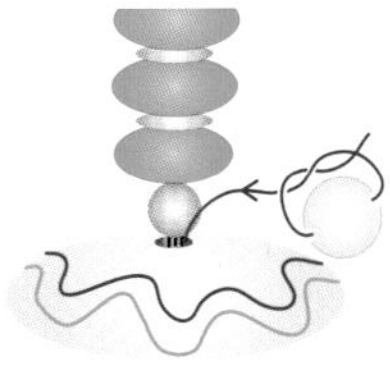

fig 4

The new thread and the old thread end are fastened off when all of the stranding for the tassel is complete. The needle has to pass through the head bead many times when making a tassel so it is important that the hole is not obstructed by knots.

Method for Beadweaving

Work the old thread until you have no less than 15cm of thread remaining. Remove the needle from this thread end and leave the end hanging loose. Prepare the needle with a new thread and tie a keeper bead 5cm from the end.

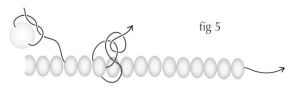

fig 5

Starting about 15 beads back from the old end of the thread pass the needle through 3 - 4 beads towards the old thread end. Make a double knot here (fig 5). Pass the needle through a further 4 - 5 beads and repeat the knot. Pass the needle through to emerge alongside the old thread end and continue the beading. When you have worked on a little you can trim away the keeper bead at the end of this thread. Return to the old thread end and reattach the needle. Finish off this end as in "Finishing off a Thread End".

Knotty Problems & Too Many Threads

When making tassels and beadweaving 3D shapes, beaded beads and fancy ropes the needle has to pass through the beads of the pattern many times.

Each time you pass through a bead the hole becomes a little more filled with thread. This can be used to the advantage of the design, as the beadwork will stiffen a little more with each extra thread pass and is ideal if you are making a 3D hollow beaded bead. However, as you continue to pass through the same beads, the holes become very congested.

If you need to continue to pass the needle through these congested beads you can swap to a finer needle or you may be able to find an alternative route through some adjacent beads. Do not force a needle through a blocked bead - you will probably break the bead and spoil the work.

The worst culprit for blocking holes in beads is a misplaced knot. Be careful where you tie your knots when adding a new thread. Do not position knots adjacent to, or inside beads, that you have to pass the needle through again. In many of the projects you will be asked to leave a thread end hanging loose and unfinished, whilst you continue with the pattern, to prevent the holes from becoming blocked. You will be instructed when to finish off these thread ends.

Following A Pattern & Bead Recipes

Read through the project before you start. It will give you an overall view of 'what goes where' and why the stages are arranged in a particular order.

Some of the materials lists at the start of the projects are quite long. This makes for an exciting combination of colours and textures in the finished project but it can be a little confusing when you first start. Make yourself a slim cardboard bookmark listing the beads A-Z with your own description of the colours and sizes, or even better, sew a few beads alongside the letters for a quick and accurate key to your bead palette.

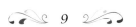

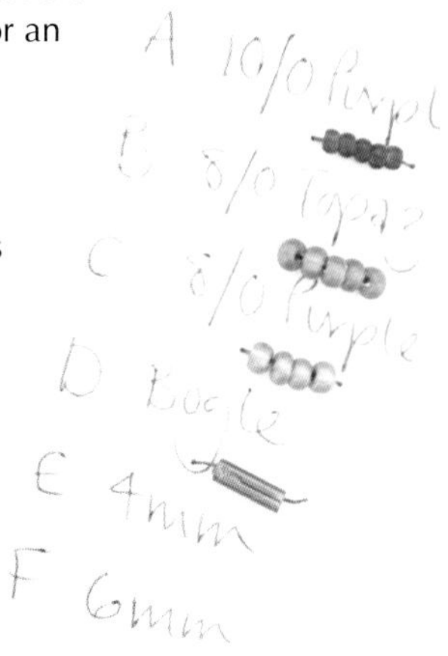

Brick Stitch for Beginners

Brick stitch is used in several different projects. If you have not used this technique before it is a good idea to make a sampler ten beads x ten rows just to familiarise yourself with how the stitch works. Try out an increase and a decrease too so you are prepared to follow the pattern accurately.

Brick stitch is so called because of the pattern the beads form as they line up, in staggered rows, giving the impression of a brick wall. It can form flat pieces or cylinders but both require a starter row or 'foundation row' onto which the first row of brick stitch is worked.

1 The Ladder Stitch Foundation Row - This ladder of beads is worked so that all the holes of the beads are lined up perpendicular to the length of the row.

Prepare the needle with 1.5m of single thread and tie a keeper bead 15cm from the end. Thread on two beads. Pass the needle back down through the first bead and up through the second to bring the two beads alongside one another (fig 1).

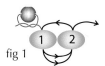 

fig 1   fig 2

2 Thread on a third bead; pass the neeedle back up bead 2 and back down bead 3 (fig 2) bringing bead 3 to sit alongside beads 1 and 2. Repeat for seven further beads to give you a row of ten (fig 3).

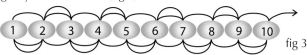

fig 3

3 Starting to Brick Stitch - Thread on two beads (11 & 12). Pick up the loop of thread between beads 10 and 9 and pass back up through bead 12 in the opposite direction (fig 4). This should bring the two new beads to sit alongside one another with bead 11 slightly overhanging the previous row.

4 Thread on bead 13. Pick up the loop of thread between beads 9 and 8 and pass back up bead 13 (fig 5). Repeat adding one bead at a time to the end of the row (ten beads in total).

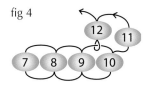 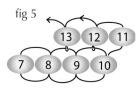

fig 4   fig 5

5 Pick up beads 21 and 22 to start the next row (fig 6) and work to the end of the row. Continue to work a further seven rows.

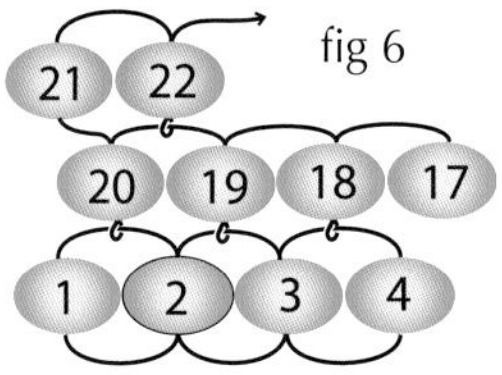

fig 6

Each row starts with a two bead stitch followed by eight single bead stitches. The beads of each row should sit right alongside one another and the rows should sit closely on top of one another. You should not be able to see the thread except at the top and bottom of the work.

You will also need to know how to shape the work by increasing and decreasing the length of the rows.

6 Decreasing at the End of the Row - A plain brick stitch row starts with a two-bead stitch. If you pick up the first loop of thread along the previous row, the new row will overhang by half of one bead (as fig 4). If you pick up the second loop along the new beads will sit half a bead in from the end of the previous row (fig 7) decreasing the row length by one bead.

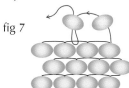

fig 7   fig 8

If you need to make a bigger decrease you can weave the needle up and down through the beads of the previous row until you are in the correct place to start the new row with a two-bead stitch (fig 8). The new two-bead stitch can stretch across two bead loops (as fig 7) if necessary, to follow the pattern correctly.

This method of repositioning the needle to start the beading in the correct position, with the needle pointing in the correct direction, to begin the stitch, is the main skill required to make a success of any brick stitch project.

7 Increasing at the End of the Row - Pick up one bead and pass the needle back up through the last bead of the row. Pass back down through the increase bead (fig 9) - this is just like making the foundation row. You can continue to add beads to the end of the row with the same method if the pattern requires it (fig 10).

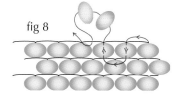

fig 9 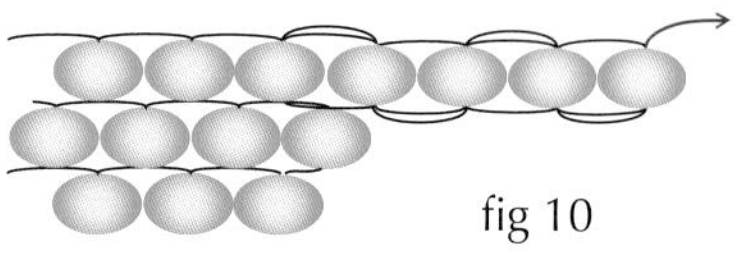   fig 10

In fig 9 the needle is emerging in the wrong direction to start the next row from the newly increased bead. Pass the needle through the previous bead of this row and start the new row with a two-bead stitch from this bead - make sure you have picked out the correct two beads for this location on the pattern. You can then backtrack to add any beads required at the start of the row above the increase bead.

If you do need to add extra beads to the start of a row you will need to work the beads that are attached to the previous row first; then backtrack up and down through the beads just added to the start of the row. Add the beads to the start of the row as above.

8 Circular Brick Stitch - To close up a circular row of brick stitch you need to join the last bead of the row to the first bead. Pass the needle down the first bead, pick up the thread loop underneath the bead and pass back up through the same bead (fig 11).

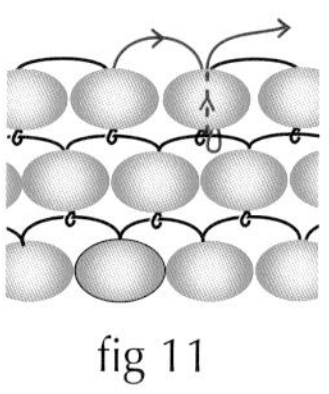

fig 11

Tassel Terminology

Passementerie is the traditional craft of making braids and tassels from silky threads and cords. To a passementier, or tassel maker, there are three basic buiding blocks for a decorative tassel - the hanging loop, the head and the stranding or skirt. As beaders, we can embellish or substitute one, two or all of these blocks with glistening crystals, glass bugles and seed beads.

The Hanging Loop

This needs to be fit for the purpose.

A lightweight design can hang from a single string of beads.
A tassel that will attach to a key or a cabinet handle will need a very strong, narrow loop.
An elaborate tassel to slip onto a silky cord to tie back a heavy curtain needs a more substantial woven or multi-stranded hanging loop.

For a light-weight curtain tieback try dividing the hanging loop in half. Put a loop at each end to slip over the tieback hooks.

The Head

The tassel top or head bead brings all of the strands of the skirt together and connects them to the hanging loop. On commercially-made tassels the head is often a turned wooden shape covered in cord or fabric.
The designs in this book will show you how to encrust large base beads with decorative beaded patterns, make hollow beaded structures, construct beaded frames around crystals and weave geometric shapes to create a treasure trove of design options.

A stretch of seed beads at the top gives the strand maximum flexibility.

The Skirt or Stranding

What a tassel is all about! The strands can be all the same length or graded in length and colour, straight or branched or shaped at the ends to form leaves, picots or loops.

To make the strand hang softly and straight you will need to be careful with the tension in your thread.

Medium-sized feature beads or weight beads are normally added towards the bottom of the strand to help it to hang well.

For a true tassel the strands should come together at a single point, if they spread out along an edge they are more properly called a fringe.

Bugle beads define each strand against its neighbour giving a clean uncluttered line within the design.

The weight beads add colour, glisten & pattern to your design.

Fringe strands
sit side-by-side along an edge.

Making A Basic Tassel

Just because the technique is simple and straightforward doesn't mean that the result will be 'run of the mill' - choose a top bead with an interesting texture or flecks, swirls or patterns in contrasting colours - then pick up those colours with your seed beads and bugles.

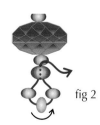

You Will Need

Materials

One 14-18mm bead for the top of the tassel
7g of size 10/0 seed beads to match the main bead A
2g of size 8/0 seed beads to tone B
2g of size 8/0 seed beads to tone C
4g of size 3 bugle beads to tone D
Seven weight beads approximately 6mm in size to tone E
Seven weight beads approximately 8mm in size to tone F
One 4mm jump ring or a 5mm split ring
A reel of size D beading thread to match the darkest tone
Two small scraps of paper approximately 15mm square

Tools

A size 10 beading needle
A pair of scissors to trim the threads

A simple tassel is made with one length of thread. The needle passes up and down through the tassel top (or head bead) adding one strand at a time.

Just above the tassel top bead the needle turns direction through a jump ring, or a large holed seed bead, so it can pass down through the tassel top bead once more to be ready to make the next strand.

Getting the bead combination correct for a tassel strand is sometimes very easy - sometimes not. For your first tassel follow these bead counts for the strands as they are in the correct proportions for a 14-18mm tassel top bead. Then try out new bead combinations, strand lengths and strand endings - it's very addictive!

1 Prepare the needle with 1.5m of single thread. Tie the jump ring 15 cm from the end of the thread with a secure double knot. Make sure the knot cannot slip through the gap in the jump ring.

2 Pierce the first paper with the needle, pass through the tassel top bead and pierce the second paper (fig 1).

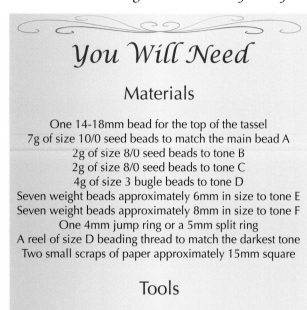

The papers stop the small seed beads from running inside the larger hole in the tassel top bead and prevents the ring from jamming into the hole at the top.

fig 1

Design Tip....

Don't use two bugle beads together on a tassel strand. The ends of these beads are always a little uneven so they will not sit perfectly against one another. Put a seed bead in-between the bugle beads for a smoother result that will hang beautifully.

3 **The First Strand** - Tassel strands hang better if you start with a length of small seed beads. The bugle beads give definition to the pattern and the weight beads should be near to the bottom.

Thread on 15A, 1D, 1A, 1B, 1A, 1D, 3A, 1C, 1E, 1C, 1A, 1F, 1A, 1B and 3A.

Leaving aside the last 3A beads threaded to anchor the strand, pass the needle back up the last B bead.

This will pull the 3A beads up into a picot at the bottom of the strand (fig 2).

fig 2

There are other options for strand endings (shown opposite) for you to try out on your own tassel designs.

Left - This tassel uses a size 6/0 seed bead at the top instead of a jump ring - it is more secure as there is no gap through which the thread might escape, but it can only connect to another thread - you cannot connect it directly to a further jump ring, a clip or a chain.

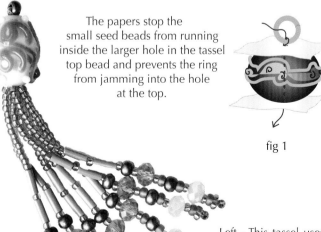

Strand Endings

At the bottom of the strand you need to form an anchor from one or more beads - the strand ending can add considerably to the design of your tassel.

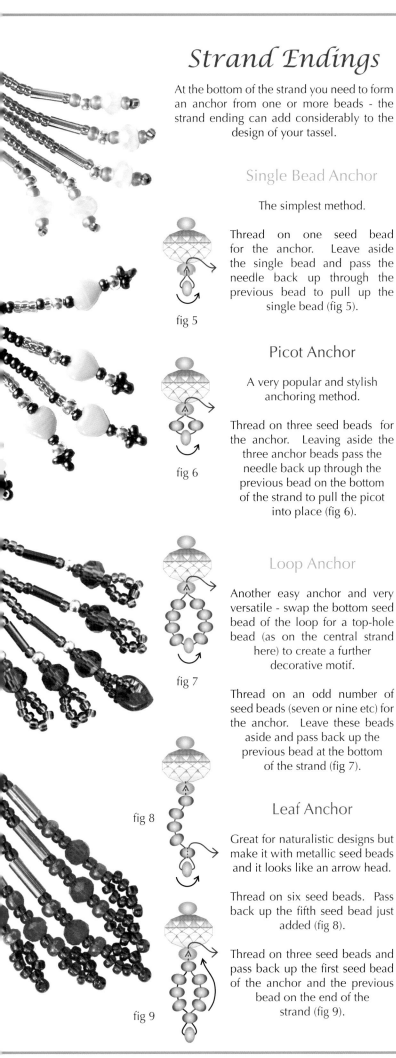

Single Bead Anchor

The simplest method.

Thread on one seed bead for the anchor. Leave aside the single bead and pass the needle back up through the previous bead to pull up the single bead (fig 5).

fig 5

Picot Anchor

A very popular and stylish anchoring method.

Thread on three seed beads for the anchor. Leaving aside the three anchor beads pass the needle back up through the previous bead on the bottom of the strand to pull the picot into place (fig 6).

fig 6

Loop Anchor

Another easy anchor and very versatile - swap the bottom seed bead of the loop for a top-hole bead (as on the central strand here) to create a further decorative motif.

Thread on an odd number of seed beads (seven or nine etc) for the anchor. Leave these beads aside and pass back up the previous bead at the bottom of the strand (fig 7).

fig 7

Leaf Anchor

Great for naturalistic designs but make it with metallic seed beads and it looks like an arrow head.

Thread on six seed beads. Pass back up the fifth seed bead just added (fig 8).

fig 8

Thread on three seed beads and pass back up the first seed bead of the anchor and the previous bead on the end of the strand (fig 9).

fig 9

4 The needle is emerging from the bottom B bead of the strand above the picot anchor. Pass the needle back up through all of the other beads of the strand.

Pierce the paper below the tassel top bead. Pass through this bead and the piece of paper above it to emerge alongside the jump ring (fig 3).

Adjust the tension in the tassel strand. It needs to be soft enough for the strand to fall naturally from the tassel top bead, but with no thread showing between the beads, or at the top of the strand.

Pass the needle through the jump ring and back down through the papers and the tassel top bead to emerge at the top of the first tassel strand (fig 4).

Check the strand tension again.

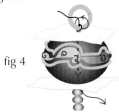

fig 4

fig 3

5 Thread a second strand to match the first. Make the picot anchor at the bottom and pass back up through the strand beads, the papers and the tassel top bead (as fig 3). Adjust the tension in the new strand if necessary.

Pass the needle through the jump ring and back down through the papers and the tassel top bead ready to begin the third tassel strand (as fig 4).

Design Tip....
Make an odd number of tassel strands - odd numbers fall into a better-shaped tassel than even numbers.

6 Repeat until you have made seven strands in total.

Finish with the needle alongside the jump ring.

Tie the needle end of the thread to the tail securely with a double knot.

Carefully tear away the papers to reveal the tassel.

Neaten the thread ends by passing both through the tassel top bead and trimming very close to the bottom of the big bead.

Dab the thread loops over the jump ring with a little clear nail polish - this will protect the threads and help to prevent them slipping through the gap in the ring.

Design Your Own Tassel

Tassel strands do not have to be straight and tassel design does not have to stop just above the tassel top bead.

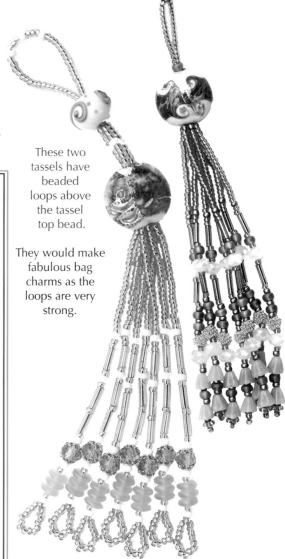

These two tassels have beaded loops above the tassel top bead.

They would make fabulous bag charms as the loops are very strong.

Pink Tassel

Start with a keeper bead 15cm from the end of your thread. Pass down through the papers and the tassel top bead. Make the first strand as usual & pass back up through the papers and the tassel top bead.

Thread on one size 6/0 seed bead (or other small bead with a big hole) and sufficient small seed beads to make your loop. Pass back down the size 6/0 seed bead, the papers and the tassel top bead ready to make the next strand.

Make the strand as before to emerge from the top of the tassel top bead. Pass the needle through the size 6/0 seed bead and the seed beads of the loop. Pass back down the size 6/0 seed bead, the papers and the tassel top bead ready to make the next strand. Repeat until you have made all of the required strands.

Finish with the needle emerging just below the size 6/0 seed bead. Remove the keeper bead and tie the needle thread to the tail with a secure double knot. Neaten both ends as step 6, page 13.

Turquoise Tassel

Make this variation in a very similar way. Here the design has three short seed bead strands between the tassel top bead and a smaller feature bead under the loop. Start with a keeper bead above the large tassel top bead and make the first tassel strand. Thread a short seed bead link to the smaller feature bead and make the seed bead loop above that. Pass back down the link and make the next tassel strand. Repeat adding a second and third link. Add the last few tassel strands passing through one of the three existing links and the bead loop at the top.

Making a Branched Strand

Branched stranding can be very effective when clustered around the top of a straight tassel or used on its own to create fronds & multi-layered cascades of beads.

For a spikey strand keep the side branches quite short, don't use weight beads and pull the thread a little tighter than normal.

1 Thread on the seed beads for the main stem. Leave aside the last bead to form the anchor and pass back up the preceeding four or five beads of the strand (fig 10).

2 Thread on four beads for the side branch. Leave aside the last bead to anchor the strand and pass back up through the first three beads of the side branch and the following four beads up the main strand (fig 11). Pull the thread through firmly.

3 Repeat step 2 to make a second side branch passing up through the next few beads of the main strand (fig 12).
Repeat until you reach the top of the main strand varying the branch length if you wish.

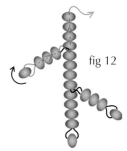

fig 10

fig 11

fig 12

Branched stranding or fringing is also called 'coralling' as it can resemble red coral when made in bright colours and pulled up a little more tightly than normal.

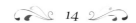

Making a Twisted Fringe Strand

Twisted strands add a simple design statement that can lift a plain piece of work with a textural contrast or accentuate the sumptuousness of a grand project.

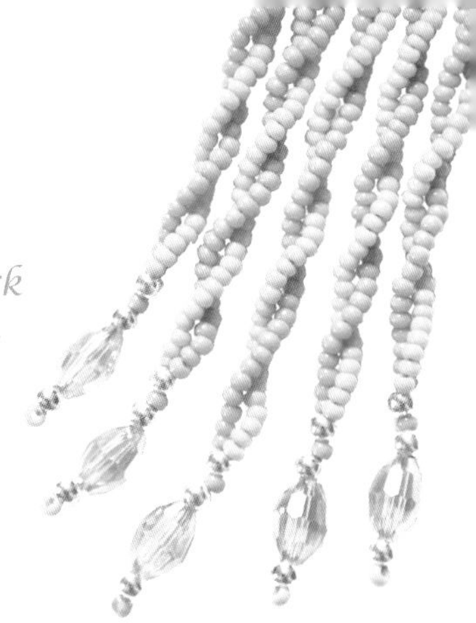

A beaded twisted strand will only hold its shape if it is anchored through two separate beads at the top edge - for this reason it is a technique best reserved for fringe style stranding and not a conventional tassel - see the Casbah Tassel project on page 24. If you would like to practice the technique make a short length of ladder stitch as in steps 1, 2 and 3 of the Moroccan Tassel on page 21 as this makes an ideal base for twisted fringe strands.

1 You need to work with a double thread if possible.
The twist will work better in smaller sized seed beads (10/0, 11/0) and Delica beads.

Pass the needle through the work to emerge from the first bead on the edge of the base row (fig 13).

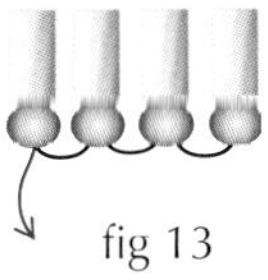

2 Thread on the seed beads for the downstrand of the twist and the decoration, if any, for the end of the strand.

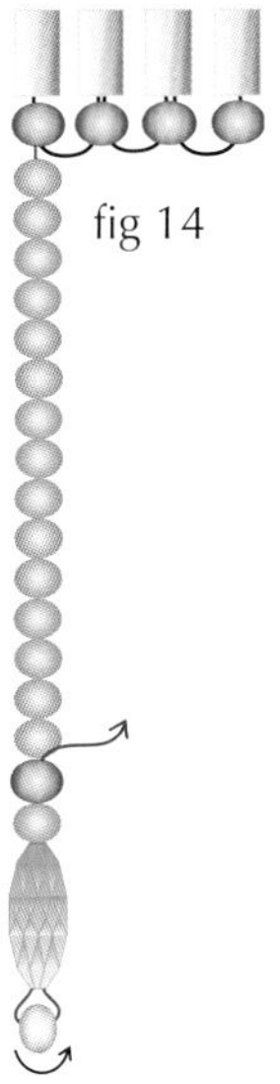

Extra Info....
The weight beads at the bottom of a twisted strand need to be kept to a minimum. The twist will have to travel through the centre of these beads which detracts from the tightness of the twists that you can achieve in the seed beads.

Make the anchor and pass back up through the weight beads ready to make the upstrand of the twist (fig 14).

Thread on the same number of seed beads as before and check the two strands are exactly the same length - if they are not adjust the bead count until they match exactly (fig 15).

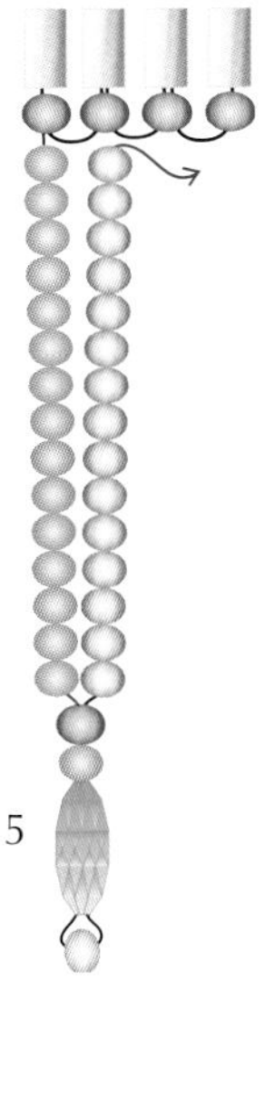

fig 13

fig 14

fig 15

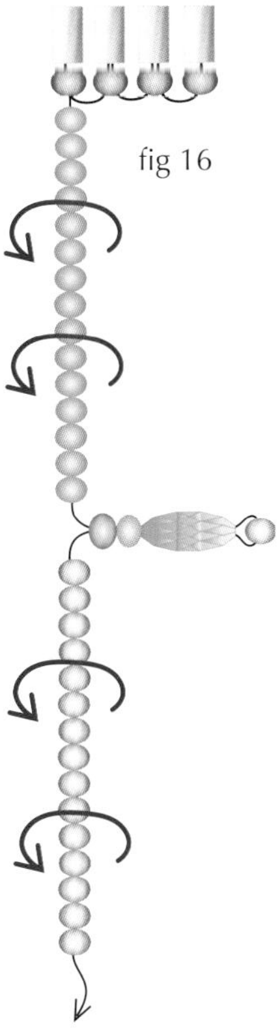

fig 16

fig 17

3 Anchor the base row of the work firmly and stretch out the two strands (as fig 16). Pinch the thread up against the last bead threaded and twist the thread by rolling it through your fingers.

The twist will start to run down through the beads and out towards the needle end of the thread. As you twist the weight beads in the middle will flip over and over transmitting the twist to the other half of the sequence. It is very important that the twists travelling towards the needle are allowed to fall out of the thread or they will counteract the twist through the beads.

4 Keeping the pinch in the thread tight against the last bead, bring the two strands parallel and allow the twist to form. If you need more twist pull the two sides apart and continue to twist the thread until the effect is satisfactory.

5 Pass the needle up through the next bead along your base row (fig 17). Pass down the next base row bead along to start the next downstrand.

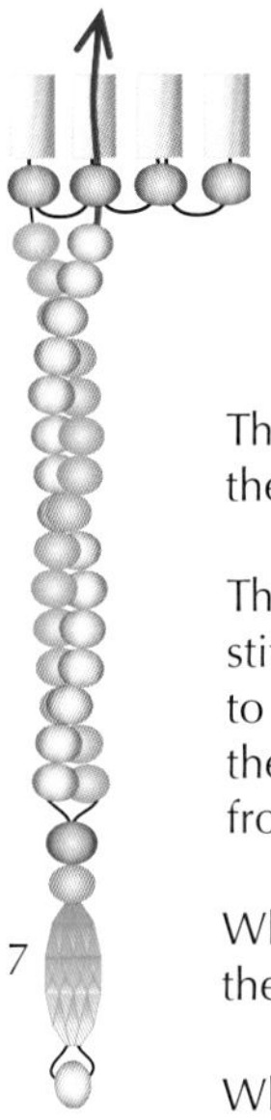

This sample is worked with two similar chalky-coloured beads.

The subtle difference between the up & down strands of the twist emphasises the technique beautifully.

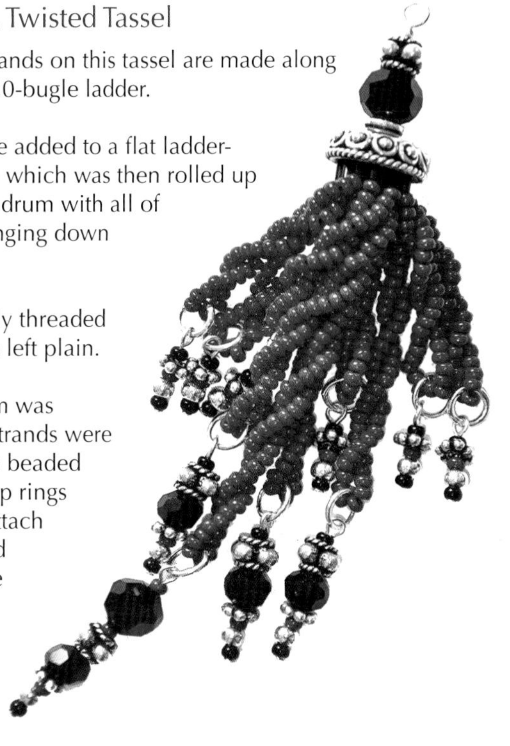

A Twisted Tassel

The twisted strands on this tassel are made along the edge of a 20-bugle ladder.

The twists were added to a flat ladder-stitched length which was then rolled up to form a little drum with all of the strands hanging down from the edge.

When originally threaded the twists were left plain.

When the drum was complete the strands were decorated with beaded headpins. Jump rings were used to attach these decorated headpins to the strand ends.

A branched strand tassel decorated with leaves and flower buds.

Here the effect is soft and flowing as the weight beads pull the strands down into a more relaxed position.

Amritsar Tassel

You Will Need

Materials

7g of size 10/0 silver lined red seed beads A
10g of size 10/0 silver lined purple seed beads B
5g of size 8/0 silver lined gold seed beads C
7g of size 3 transparent purple AB bugle beads D
Seven 6mm purple fire polished faceted beads E
Twenty-seven 6mm red fire polished faceted beads F
Seven 8mm purple fire polished faceted beads G
Seven 4mm red fire polished faceted beads H
One 4mm gold plated jump ring
A reel of purple size D beading thread

Tools

A size 10 beading needle
A size 13 beading needle
A pair of scissors to trim the threads

*The finished length of this tassel is 22cm
including the hanging loop.
It measures 15cm below the hanging loop.*

Inspired by traditional Indian jewellery designs this tassel is based on a stack of beaded drums. The largest drum is made from six separate tassels with a further tassel dangling from the centre to taper the shape. This is good choice for a first tassel project, as lots of simple techniques build up into a spectacular design.

This Tassel is Made in Five Stages
The large drum.
The central tassel.
The medium drum.
The small drum.
The hanging loop.

1 The Large Drum - The large drum is made from 7G beads.

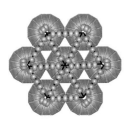

Fig 1 shows the top view of the large drum when complete with 1G bead surrounded by 6G beads.

The 6G beads around the edge of the drum support eighteen tassel strands in total. These tassel strands need to be made before the drum is assembled.

fig 1

2 Prepare the size 10 needle with 1.5m of thread and tie a keeper bead 15cm from the end.

Thread on 1G, 16A, 1B, 1A, 1B, 1D, 1B, 1C, 1B, 1D, 1B, 1C, 3B, 1A, 1B, 1C, 1A, 1F, 1A, 1C and 3B.

Leaving aside the last 3B threaded to anchor the strand pass the needle back up the other beads of the strand to emerge at the far side of the G bead (fig 2).

Thread on 1A and 3B. Pass the needle back down the A bead to pull the 3B beads into a picot. Pass the needle down through the G bead (fig 3).

fig 2

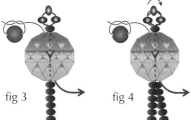

fig 3   fig 4

3 Thread on 16A, 1B, 1A, 1B, 1D, 1B, 1C, 1B, 1D, 1B, 1C, 3B, 1A, 1B, 1C, 1A, 1F, 1A, 1C and 3B. Make an anchor from the 3B beads and pass back up the strand as before to emerge from the G bead at the top.

Pass the needle up through the A bead above the G bead; through the 3B beads of the picot and back down the A and G beads to turn the needle ready to make the next strand (fig 4).

Make the third tassel strand to match the first two. Pass the needle up through the G bead to complete the strand.

Finish off both of the thread ends neatly and securely without blocking the holes in the G bead or the A bead above it.

Repeat to make five more identical tassels.

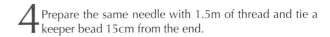

4 Prepare the same needle with 1.5m of thread and tie a keeper bead 15cm from the end.

* Select one of the tassels made in steps 2 and 3.

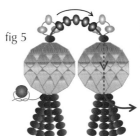
fig 5

Pass the needle up through the G bead at the top of this tassel and the A bead at the base of the picot.

Thread on 5B. Pass the needle down through the A bead at the top of a second tassel and the G bead below it (fig 5).

Thread on 5B. Pass the needle up through the G bead of the first tassel and the A bead above it.

Pass the needle through the first 3B of the 5B between this tassel and the next (fig 6).

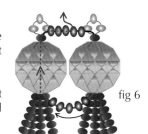
fig 6

5 Thread on 2B, 1A, 1C, 1A and 2B. Pass the needle through the middle B bead of the bottom strap between the G beads (fig 7).

fig 7   fig 8

Pass the needle back up the last four of the seven beads just added to emerge at the far side of the C bead.

Thread on 3A. Pass the needle up through the C bead again to bring the 3A into a strap to the side of the C bead (fig 8).

fig 9

Thread on 3A. Pass the needle up through the C bead and the following three beads to bring the 3A into a strap to the other side of the C bead. Pass the needle through the middle bead of the strap between the two G beads and the following 2B to point towards the second of the G beads (fig 9).

Pass the needle down the A bead at the top of the G bead and the G bead below it to emerge from the bottom of the second G bead.

6 Repeat from the * in step 4 to add a third G bead tassel to the second G bead. The needle is pointing down from the second G bead and not up as in fig 5, so you will need to reverse the 'ups and downs' to connect this link to the last one.

Repeat to add the fourth, fifth and sixth G bead tassels to give you a line of six G bead tassels. Join the sixth G bead to the first one with a matching link to make a ring. On the last stitch of this last link bring the needle up through the first G bead only and not through the A bead above it.

The seventh G bead now needs to be secured in the centre of the ring. You will need to pull the thread quite tightly to make the drum firm.

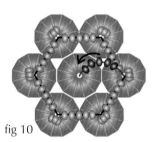

7 Place the seventh G bead in the centre of the ring. Thread on 5B.

Pass the needle down the hole in the centre G bead (fig 10).

fig 10

Thread on 5B and pass the needle up through the first G bead.

Pass the needle through the 5B strap to the centre G bead and down through the centre G bead.

8 Thread on 5B. Pass the needle up through the next G bead of the ring. Thread on 5B and pass the needle down through the centre G bead.

Repeat for all the G beads around the drum to join all of the G beads to one another.

Do not fasten off the thread ends - leave them loose and remove the needle.

Extra Info....

In this design the needle has to pass through some beads many times and the holes can become congested with thread. You can swap to the finer (size 13) needle when the holes become tight but more importantly do not finish any thread ends with a knot in any areas that are still to be worked.

9 The Central Tassel - This seven-stranded tassel uses an F bead to bring all the strands together instead of a G bead as before.

Prepare the size 10 needle with 2m of single thread. Tie the 4mm jump ring securely 15cm from the end of the thread.

Thread on 1F, 28B, 1A, 1C, 1A, 3D, 1B, 1C, 1B, 1D, 1B, 1C, 4B, 1A, 1C, 1A, 1E, 1A, 1C and 3B. Leave the last 3B aside to anchor the strand and pass the needle back up through the other beads to emerge through the top of the F bead.

Pass the needle through the jump ring and back down the F bead ready to start the next tassel strand.

Make a second tassel strand to match the first strand. Pass through the jump ring at the top and back down the F bead to begin the third strand.

Repeat to complete seven identical strands in total. Finish the thread ends neatly and securely.

This tassel is now linked to the large drum.

10 Re-attach the same needle to the thread end from step 8. If necessary pass the needle through the beads of the drum to emerge from the bottom of the central G bead.

Pass the needle through the jump ring at the top of the central tassel and back up through the central G bead taking care not to allow the thread to slip through the tiny gap in the jump ring (fig 11). Thread on 1A, 1D and 1A.

Pass the needle back down the D bead, the first A bead and the G bead once more to leave a spur sticking up from the top of the drum (fig 12). This will connect to the medium drum in due course.

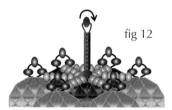

fig 11

fig 12

Pass the needle through the jump ring at the top of the central tassel again and back up through the central G bead. Pass the needle through the A and D beads of the spur and back down the G bead to make the connections stronger. Repeat once more.

Although the G beads of the drum are all connected together the drum will not feel firm to the touch - you now need to reinforce the work with additional passes of the needle.

Swap the size 10 needle for the finer size 12 needle. Pass the needle through all of the 5B links again pulling the thread firmly - repeat until the needle will not pass through the beads again - the drum will feel much more firm.

Finish off the thread ends neatly and securely.

11 The Medium Drum - Prepare the size 10 needle with 1.5m of thread and tie a keeper bead 15cm from the end. Thread on 1F, 4B, 1F and 4B. Pass the needle up through the first F bead once more to bring the F beads parallel to one another (fig 13).

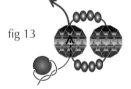

fig 13

fig 14

Pass the needle through the following 4B and 1F beads (fig 14) and thread on 4B, 1F and 4B.

Pass the needle through the second F bead of the first stitch; the following 4B and the third F bead of the row (fig 15).

Repeat to add a further 3F beads (6F in total).

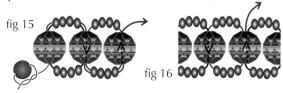

fig 15

fig 16

Join the sixth F bead to the first with two straps of 4B (fig 16).

12 Before you add the seventh F bead in the middle of the drum the outside of the 6F ring is decorated with straps of seed beads.

Pass the needle through the first 3B beads of the closest 4B strap. Thread on 1B, 1A, 1C, 1A and 1B.

Pass the needle through the middle 2B beads on the strap at the bottom of the drum.
Turn the needle and pass it back up through the five beads just added. Pass the needle through the last three beads of the 4B strap at the top in the same direction as before (fig 17).

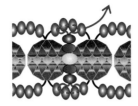

fig 17

Pass the needle through the first 3B beads of the next 4B strap along and repeat to add a second decorative strap in the gap between the two F beads. Repeat to make six straps in total.

13 Reposition the needle to emerge from an F bead and thread on 3B. Place 1F in the centre of the drum and pass the needle down through this F bead. Thread on 3B and pass up through the F bead on the edge of the drum once more to make the first connection to the central drum bead.

Referring to step 7 connect the remaining 5F beads around the edge of the drum to the central F bead with straps of 3B beads. Finish with the needle emerging from the central F bead.

14 Pass the needle through the top A bead of the spur at the top of the tassel drum. Turn the needle and pass it back up through the centre F bead of the new drum.

The connection between the large drum and the medium drum is now reinforced with a ring of short strands between the F beads of the medium drum and the picots around the top of the large drum.

15 Pass the needle through one of the radiating 3B strands and down through the following F bead. Thread on 1B, 1A, 1C, 1A and 1B. Pass the needle through the top B bead of the closest picot on the large drum. Pass the needle back up the five beads just added and the F bead on the medium drum.

Pass the needle through the 4B link along the top edge to the next F bead of the medium drum and repeat.

Repeat four more times to add six links in total. Leave the thread end loose and remove the needle.

16 The Small Drum - Referring to step 11 make an outer ring of 6H beads using 3B beads to make each link. Place 1H in the centre of the ring and secure into place as in step 13 with stitches of 2B. Finish with the needle emerging from the central H bead.

17 Thread on 1B, 1A, 1C, 1A and 1B. Pass the needle down the centre E bead of the medium drum and through the A bead at the top of the spur from the large drum. Pass the needle back up through the medium drum, the five beads just added and the central H bead of the small drum.
Leave the thread end loose and remove the needle.

18 The Hanging Loop - Prepare the size 13 needle with 1m of double thread and tie a keeper bead 15cm from the end.

Pass the needle up through the centre H bead of the small drum to emerge alongside the previous thread end.

Thread on 1B, 1A, 1C, 1A, 1B, 1F, 1B, 1A, 1C and 1A (fig 18). These beads form the link to the base of the loop.

Thread on 12B, 1A, 1C and 1A.

Repeat this sequence until the loop is of the desired size finishing with 12B to even up the repeat.

fig 18

Pass the needle down through the beads of the strand at the base of the loop to emerge at the top of the small drum.

Pass the needle down through the central H bead of the small drum; the beads of the link to the medium drum; the central F bead of the medium drum and the 1A at the top of the spur above the large drum.

Pass the needle back up through all of these beads to emerge at the top of the small drum.

Pass the needle through the sequence above the small drum and the beads of the loop to strengthen it.

Finish off this thread end and all the remaining thread ends neatly and securely.

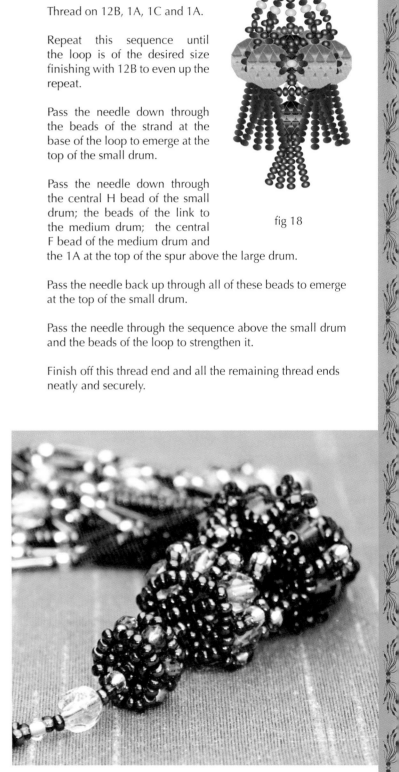

Moroccan Tassel

You Will Need

Materials

10g of size 10/0 green scarab seed beads A
4g of size 3 purple scarab bugle beads B
5g of size 10/0 silver lined gold seed beads C
One 12mm green fire polished faceted bead D
Six 6mm purple fire polished faceted beads E
Fifteen 3mm gold metallic round beads F
A reel of black size D beading thread

Tools

A size 13 beading needle
A pair of scissors to trim the threads
Clear drying nail polish

The finished length of this tassel is 23cm including the hanging loop.
It measures 18cm below the hanging loop.

At noon cross the threshold of many buildings in Morocco and you step from white, bright sunlight into cool, shady blackness. As your eyes adjust the colours grow on your conciousness - jewel-coloured tiles cover the walls and the floors with repeating mathematical patterns and calligraphic splendour.

This Tassel is Made in Three Stages

The large diamond is made with a combination of ladder stitch and brick stitch. If you have not used brick stitch before will find it useful to refer to page 10.
The fringe strands below the diamond are added.
The hanging loop which incorporates the smaller diamond is added at the top.

1 The Diamond - Prepare the needle with 2m of single thread and tie a keeper bead 15cm from the end. Thread on 1A, 1B, 2A, 1B and 1A. Pass the needle up through the first three beads and down through the second three beads to make an oblong and start the first ladder stitch section (fig 1).

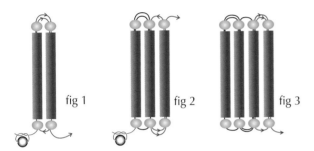

fig 1   fig 2   fig 3

2 Thread on 1A, 1B and 1A. Pass the needle down through the previous three beads to bring the new beads up parallel. Pass the needle up through the new beads (fig 2). Thread on 1A, 1B and 1A and repeat to give you four bugles in a row with A beads at either end of each bugle bead (fig 3).

3 Thread on 1A. Pass the needle down through the end A bead of the last stitch and up through the new A bead (fig 4).

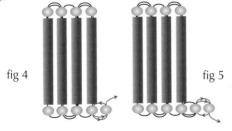

fig 4   fig 5

Repeat to attach a second A bead to the first one (fig 5).

4 Pass back up through the first lone A bead and thread on 1A and 1C. Pick up the thread loop between the two A beads and pass back up through the C bead just added (fig 6). This is the start of the first brick stitch section. Thread on 1A and pass down the last A bead of the first row (fig 7).

5 Pass the needle up through the first A bead of the first row and the first A bead of the second row (fig 8).

6 Thread on 1A and 1C; pick up the thread loop between the A and C beads of the previous row and pass back up the new C bead to start the row with a two-bead stitch (fig 9).

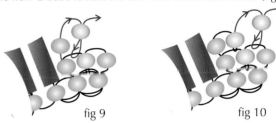

fig 9   fig 10

Thread on 1C. Pick up the thread loop between the C and A beads at the end of the previous row and pass back up through the new C bead (fig 10).

Thread on 1A and pass the needle down through the A beads at the end of the previous two rows and back up the A beads at the beginning of the rows (fig 11).

fig 11

7 Thread on 1A and 1C. As before pick up the thread loop between the A and C beads of the previous row and pass back up through the new C bead (fig 12).

fig 12   fig 13

Thread on 1A; pick up the thread loop between the two C beads on the previous row and back up through the new A bead (fig 13). Add the last two beads of the row as before.

Following fig 14 work three more rows - begin each row by passing the needle up through the first column of A beads, and add one more A bead to the centre of each row to expand the triangle and finishing with 1A.

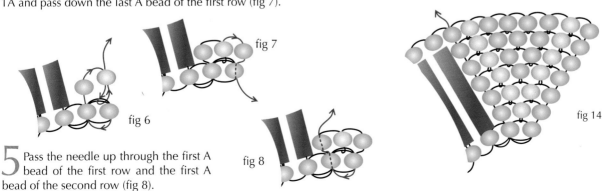

fig 6   fig 7   fig 8   fig 14

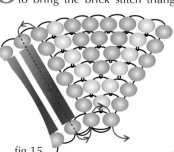

8 Pass the needle down through the 1A, 1B and 1A beads to bring the brick stitch triangle up against the bugle ladder (see fig 15). Pass the needle up through the first A bead at the base of the triangle and down through the second (fig 15).

fig 15

fig 16

9 Thread on 1A, 1B and 1A and pass the needle down through the end vertical row of A beads to bring the new bugle into place alongside the brick stitch triangle ready to start the new bugle ladder (fig 16).

10 Pass the needle up through the new A, B and A beads and add three new A, B and A bead stitches as in figs 1, 2 and 3. You will then be in the correct position to start the second brick stitch triangle.

Work the next brick stitch triangle as in figs 4 to 16.

To complete the diamond add two more ladder and brick stitch sections.

Join up the diamond by threading up the first A, B, A combination of the first ladder and down the last vertical row of A beads from the last brick stitch triangle. Bring the needle back up the A, B, A combination to emerge at the outside edge of the diamond.

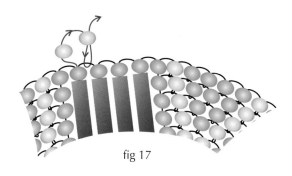

fig 17

11 The diamond has a single-row brick stitch edge. Thread on 2C and pick up the thread loop between the 2A beads along the top of the B beads (see fig 17). Pass the needle back up the second C bead to complete the first two-bead stitch (fig 17).

Work four single brick stitches in C and five stitches in A.
Work seven single brick stitches in C and five in A.
Work seven single brick stitches in C and five in A.
Work seven single brick stitches in C and five in A.
Work two stitches in C.

Pass the needle down through the first C bead, hook the needle underneath the loop of thread beneath it and pass back up through the first C. This completes the edging - do not pull the thread too tightly or you will pucker the shape of the diamond.

Finish off the thread end neatly and securely.

12 The Fringe Strands - Prepare the needle with 2m of single thread and attach to the diamond so that the needle emerges through the central A bead at the outer edge of one of the brick stitch triangles - this is the position for the central tassel strand.

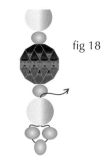

Thread on 30A, *1B, 1A, 1C, 1A, 2B, 1A, 2C, 1A, 1F, 1A, 2C, 8A, 1F, 1A, 1E, 1A, 1F and 3A.

fig 18

Leaving aside the last 3A beads threaded pass the needle back up the F bead to draw the 3A into a picot to anchor the strand (fig 18).

Pass the needle up through the rest of the beads of the tassel strand to emerge from the A bead on the edge of the dia-mond where you started the strand. Adjust the tension in the thread through the strand so that it falls softly but no thread shows between the beads**.

13 Pass the needle down through the adjacent A bead on the edge of the diamond to be in the correct position to start the second tassel strand. Thread on 21A followed by * to ** in step 12.

For the last tassel strand on this side of the centre pass the needle down through the next A bead along the diamond edge and thread on 14A followed by * to ** in step 12.

Repeat step 13 to make two further strands to the other side of the long central strand.

14
The Hanging Loop - Prepare the needle with 2m of single thread and tie a keeper bead 1m from the end. The hanging loop starts with a brick stitched diamond (see fig 19).

Work the six beads across the centre of fig 19 in ladder stitch as the foundation row.

Brick stitch up to the top of the diamond. Leave the thread end attached and remove the needle.

Remove the keeper bead and attach the needle to this end of the thread. Brick stitch with this thread to the bottom of the diamond (fig 19). Leave the needle attached.

fig 19

15
The small diamond is now joined to the top of the larger diamond. Thread on 2A, 1D and 1A. Pass the needle through the central A bead at the edge of the top of the large diamond.

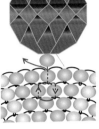

Work the needle through the next row of the large diamond to turn it around so you can pass it back up through the A bead on the edge of the large diamond (fig 20).

Pass the needle up through the beads just added to emerge at the bottom of the small diamond. Leave the thread end loose and remove the needle.

fig 20

16
Re-attach the needle to the thread end at the top of the small diamond.

Thread on 1A, 1E, 1A and sufficient A beads to make the loop to the desired size. Pass the needle back down the single A above the E bead, the E bead and the following A just above the small diamond.

You now need to strengthen the loop and the connection to the large diamond.

17
Pass the needle down through the edge beads on one side of the diamond. Rethread the needle onto the other end of the thread and repeat up the other side of the diamond (fig 21).

Pass the needle up through the A, E and A beads above the small diamond and through the A beads of the hanging loop to strengthen the top of the beading. Finish off the thread securely between the beads above the small diamond.

Re-attach the needle to the thread below the small diamond and take it downwards through the D bead and into the beads at the top of the large diamond to strengthen the join.

Finish off the thread end neatly and securely.

18
The large diamond will be quite soft to the touch so it will need to be stiffened.

Working in a well ventilated space place a plastic bag on top of a piece of corrugated cardboard or expanded polystyrene - place the diamond on the plastic.

Using ordinary dressmaking pins, pin out the diamond so that it sits in the correct shape and absolutely flat. Using clear nail polish thinly paint the surface of the beads so that the polish trickles down between the beads and onto the thread. Leave to dry thoroughly and repeat with a second coat leaving to dry again. Flip the diamond over and repeat.

If you wish you can repeat with the smaller diamond motif but, as it is much more compact, it is more stable and should not require further attention.

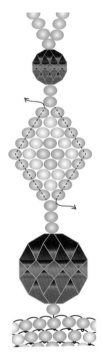

fig 21

Moroccan Inspirations
Agadir Necklace

Chalky-coloured seed beads teamed with Indian-silver style beads turn the Moroccan Tassel into a necklace for a summer beach party.

The diamond is turned 45° so it hangs as a square with the fringe strands coming from the B bead side of the motif.

The side straps attach to the triangles at the two top corners with the four strands reaching right around to the clasp at the back.

The Indian-style silver scrolled hook is attached with beaded loops.

Moroccan Inspirations
Casbah Tassel

Adding crystal beads, longer bugle beads and a twisted fringe makes the Moroccan Tassel into a Moorish extravaganza of opulence.

Materials

12g of size 10/0 purple scarab seed beads A
6g of size 5 silver lined gold twisted bugle beads B
7g of size 10/0 silver lined teal seed beads C
4g of size 10/0 silver lined capri blue seed beads D
6g of size 10/0 silver lined dark gold seed beads E
7g of size 3 silver lined capri blue bugle beads F
Nineteen 4mm blue scarab crystal beads G
Fourteen 4mm purple crystal beads H
Seven 6x4mm emerald crystal rondelle beads J
Seven 8mm purple crystal beads K
Seven 6mm bronze crystal beads L
Seven 6x8mm blue scarab crystal rondelle beads M
One 8mm blue scarab crystal bead N
One 4mm emerald crystal bead P
A reel of black size D beading thread

*The finished length of this tassel is 31cm including the hanging loop.
It measures 25cm from the top of the peacock motif just below the hanging loop.*

The Tassel is Made in Four Stages
The five sided lozenge.
The twisted fringe strands.
The decorative dangles at the bottom of the twisted fringes.
The hanging loop.

The Casbah Tassel is made in a similar fashion to the Moroccan Tassel but with a five-sided lozenge and additional detailing which extends the basic technique.

19 The Lozenge - Referring back to steps 1 and 2 complete an A and B bead ladder six bugles long.

20 Fig 22 shows the brick stitch corner pattern.

Following steps 3, 4, 5 and 6 work the first three rows of brick stitch with A and C beads.

Referring to fig 22 work the fourth row with 1A, 1C, 1D, 1C and 1A.

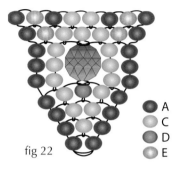

fig 22

- A
- C
- D
- E

21 The next row needs to be much deeper to accommodate the first G bead - it will be worked in 3-drop brick stitch.

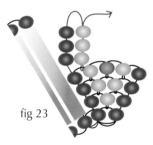

fig 23

Thread on 3A and 3C. Pick up the thread between the first A and C beads of the previous row and pass back up through the 3C beads (fig 23).

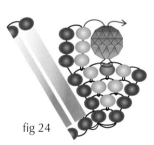

fig 24

Thread on 1G. Pick up the thread loop just before the D bead on the previous row and the thread loop just after the D bead before passing back up through the D bead (fig 24).

Adjust the tension carefully so the G bead stands vertically on top of the D bead below it.

22 Thread on 3C. Pick up the thread between the next C and A beads along the previous row and pass back up the 3C to make a single three-drop brick stitch. Thread on 3A.

Pass the needle down through the A beads at the end of previous four rows and up the A beads at the beginning of the rows as before.

23 Start the sixth row with 1A and 1E and stitch as before. Thread on 1C. The stitch between the C and G beads on the previous row has left a long thread showing between the tops of the beads - for this stitch pick up the loop quite close to the C bead. Pass back up the new C bead to complete the stitch.

Thread on 1C. Pick up the thread loop just before the G bead on the previous row and the loop just after the G bead - pass the needle up through the new C bead (fig 25).

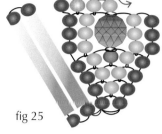

fig 25

The new C bead should sit directly on top of the G bead.

Work the remainder of the row with 1C, 1E and 1A.

Pass the needle down through the A beads at the ends of the previous rows and up through the A beads at the start of the rows as before.

24 Referring to fig 22 start the seventh row with 1A and 1E as before. Make single brick stitches with 1A, 1C, 1C, 1A and 1E. Finish the row with 1A. Reposition the needle as before to emerge through the first A bead of the row just completed.

25 To draw the curved shape of the brick stitch section up alongside the straight bugle of the ladder section an extra A bead needs to be added to the top row.

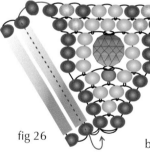

fig 26

Thread on 1A. Pass the needle down through the last 1A, 1B and 1A of the ladder section (fig 26).

Pass the needle back up through the first 8A beads at the start of the rows to emerge 1A bead below the top of the brick stitch.

Pass the needle through the extra A bead and down through the 1B of the ladder (fig 27). The extra A bead should pull snugly into the gap.

fig 27

Pass the needle through the A bead at the bottom of the ladder.

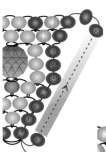

26 Following fig 15 pass the needle through the work to be ready to start the next ladder section. Thread on 1A, 1B and 2A.

Pass the needle down through the edge A beads of the brick stitch section (fig 28).

fig 28

Pass the needle back up through the first 1A and 1B just added.

fig 29

Pass the needle through the second A bead along (the 'extra' A bead), down through the second A bead from the top at the edge of the brick stitch and the following A beads (fig 29) to emerge from the bottom A bead (as fig 28). Both sides of the brick stitch section now match one another.

Pass the needle up through the first ladder stitch of 1A, 1B and 1A.

Add five more ladder stitches to this section (6B in total).

27 Repeat steps 20 to 26 inclusive to add a brick stitch section and a 6B ladder section.

Repeat steps 20 to 25 inclusive to add one more brick stitch section.

You will now have three ladder and brick stitch repeats.

28 In order to shape the work the extra A bead between the brick stitch section and the ladder needs to swap to the inside edge of the beadwork.

Reposition the needle as before (as fig 15) and thread on 2A, 1B and 1A.

Pass the needle down the edge A beads of the brick stitch section as before to emerge one A bead above the bottom (fig 30).

fig 30

Pass the needle through the extra A bead and up through the B bead (fig 31) and the following A bead at the top of the ladder.

fig 31

29 Make one ladder stitch with 1A, 1B and 1A only - this is the top of the lozenge.

To start the next brick stitch section thread on 3A. Stitch the last 2A together to start the next brick stitch section (fig 32) leaving the first 1A to be the extra A bead to mirror the 1A added in step 28.

fig 32

Work the remainder of the brick stitch section as before.

Link the top of this brick stitch section to the previous ladder stitch as a mirror image of figs 30 and 31.

30 Make one more six bead ladder section and a final brick stitch section as in steps 20 to 25 with the extra A bead on the outer edge once again.

Link the last brick stitch section to the first ladder stitch section to close up the lozenge - do not forget the extra A bead on the outside edge when you make the join.

Pass the needle through the work to emerge from one of the beads on the outside edge of the lozenge.

31 The lozenge has a single-row brick stitch edge which is enhanced with an additional short section above each of the five corners.

fig 33

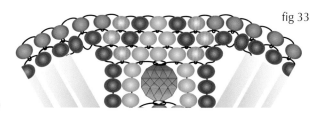

Fig 33 shows the sequence for the single row. A block of 1E, 1A, 1C, 1A and 1E is centred above each of the brick stitch corners - the remainder of the row is worked with D beads. With reference to fig 17, fig 33 and your current needle position, work the single row of brick stitch all the way around the lozenge. Link the first bead to the last bead by passing down through the first bead of the sequence.

32 If necessary, reposition the needle so it emerges through the top of the closest E bead on the outside edge of the lozenge. Thread on 1E and 1A.

Pick up the loop between the A bead and the adjacent C bead on the previous row and pass back up the new 1A to start a new row with a two bead stitch. Complete the row with two single stitches of 1A and 1E (fig 34).

fig 34

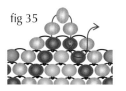

fig 35

Pass the needle down through the previous 1A and up through the first A of the short row. Thread on 3E. Pass the needle down the second A bead to draw the 3E into a small point (fig 35).

Repeat step 32 on three of the remaining four corners - leave the corner opposite the two bugle ladder until last as this is where the fringing will hang from. Work this last corner up to the end of fig 34 and finish off the thread end neatly and securely away from the edge of the work.

33

The Twisted Fringe Strands - These are made in two parts - the twist and the decorative dangle. Refer to the extra information about twisted fringes on page 14 before moving on.

Prepare the needle with 1.2m of double thread. Attach to the work and bring the needle through to emerge on the outside edge of the lozenge from one of the 2A beads added in fig 34 on the corner opposite the 2B ladder.

Thread on 60A, 1E, 1C, 1G, 1C and 3E. Leaving aside the last 3E to anchor the strand, pass the needle back up through the 1C, 1G, 1C and 1E (fig 36).

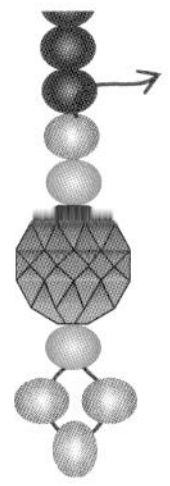

Thread on 60A.

Pinching the thread very firmly adjacent to the last A bead twist the thread in your fingers - allow the twist to travel through the stranded beads and down towards the needle. Twist 15-20 times.

Bring the two 60A sections parallel to one another - they will twist together - if there is not sufficient twist separate the strands and add more twists to the thread. Repeat until you have a satisfactory twisted bead rope.

Make sure you are pinching on tight to the twists against the last A bead. Let all of the twist between this pinch and the needle end of the thread fall out (if you don't allow this part of the thread to un-twist it will counteract the twist in the thread through the beads and the effect will not work).

Pass the needle through the adjacent A bead on the edge of the lozenge.

fig 36

34

You need to make three more twisted strands to either side of the central strand - each strand will need the same decorative end as in fig 36.

Each strand hangs between two adjacent beads on the edge of the lozenge (fig 37).

Make strand 2 with 50A beads above the first E bead - you will need 51 beads on the return strand to accommodate the stepped edge.

Make strand 3 with 40 A above the first E bead.

Make strand 4 with 30A above the first E bead.

Repeat the last three strands to the other side of the central strand.

Finish off the thread end neatly and securely.

fig 37

35

The Decorative Dangles - Prepare the needle with 1m of double thread and tie a keeper bead 15cm from the end. Thread on 1M, 1H ,1E and 3C. Leaving the 3C aside to anchor the strand pass the needle back up through the 1E, 1H and 1M beads.

Thread on 11C. Pass the needle through the 3C beads of the anchor and thread on 11C.

Pass the needle back down the 1M, 1H and 1E beads (fig 38).

Pass the needle through the 3C beads of the anchor and back up the 1E , 1H and 1M beads.

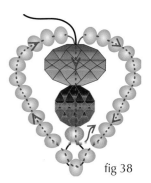

fig 38

Thread on 2C, 1L, 1C, 1D, 1E, 1K, 1E, 1J, 1E, 3A, 1E, 1G, 1C, 1B, 1D, 1E, 1D, 1H and 1C. Pass the needle through the middle 1E bead of the 3E anchor at the bottom of the first twisted strand made in step 33. Thread on 1C and pass the needle down through the H bead to draw this section up to the bottom of the twist (fig 39). Pass the needle down through the remaining beads of the new section. Re-inforce the 11C frame around the beads at the bottom of the strand and finish off the thread ends neatly and securely.

fig 39

Repeat step 35 to add a decorative finishing sequence to each of the other six twisted strands.

36 The Hanging Loop - With reference to the previous techniques work the bottom five rows of the brick stitch grid (fig 40) using 1.5m of single thread. The next row is worked in five-drop brick stitch to accomodate the larger N bead.

Referring to step 21 work the first stitch with 5A and 5C. Add 1N bead to the middle of the row and finish with one stitch of 5C and one of 5A.

The following row starts with 1A and 1C as before.

The long thread loop between the C and N beads on the previous row will support two 1C bead stitches.

You will be able to fit in a central 1C above the N bead (as fig 25) and two more C beads along the second long thread loop.

Finish this row with 1C and 1A.

Work the last three rows as fig 40. Finish with the thread emerging from one of the A beads on the top row.

Thread on 3A, 1H and 3A.

Pass the needle down the last A bead on the top row (fig 41).

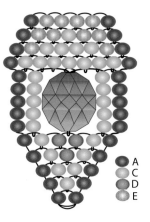

A
C
D
E

fig 40

fig 41

Pass the needle up through the adjacent 1E on the top row and thread on 3A, 1H and 3A.

Pass the needle down through the third E bead along to make a second loop which is a little narrower at the base than the first loop (fig 42).

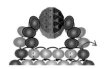

fig 42

Reinforce these two loops several times as these form the link to the hanging strap itself. Finish off this thread end neatly and securely.

Attach the lower tip of this brick stitched section to the top of the lozenge with a sequence of 1E, 1P and 1E. Make the connection strong, adding additional E beads if necessary.

37 The strap is made in ladder stitch. Prepare the needle with 1.5m of double thread and tie a keeper bead 15cm from the end.

Thread on 1C, 1F, 1C, 1E, 1F and 1E.

Make the first stitch as in fig 1.

Make the next stitch with 1C, 1F and 1C and the following stitch with 1E, 1F and 1E. (fig 43).

Repeat to make 41 alternating stitches in total.

The edges of this ladder are enhanced with a brick stitch picot.

fig 43

38 The needle will be emerging from an edge bead. Thread on 3A. Pick up the first thread loop along the strap edge and pass back up through the third A bead (fig 44).

 fig 44    fig 45

Thread on 2A. Pick up the next thread loop along and pass back up the second A bead just added (fig 45). Repeat to the end of this edge. Repeat the same pattern down the other edge of the strap.

Pass through the last ladder stitch and thread on 1E, 1A and 1C. Pass through the first H bead added in step 36. Thread on 1C, 1A and 1E and pass through this end of the strap again in the same direction as before. Reinforce this stitch.

Repeat to connect the other end of the strap to the other H bead to complete the beading.

Finish off all remaining thread ends neatly and securely.

Follow the directions in step 18 to stiffen the main lozenge and the N bead feature - keep the polish away from the surface of the crystal beads or they will spoil.

Persian Tassel

You Will Need

Materials

5g of size 11/0 silver lined teal seed beads A
5g of size 8/0 silver lined bronze AB seed beads B
5g of DB610 silver lined violet Delica beads C
Twenty-five 3mm purple fire polished faceted beads D
Twenty-five 4mm blue scarab fire polished faceted beads E
Five 4mm copper capri fire polished faceted beads F
Six 6mm copper capri fire polished faceted beads G
One 6mm teal fire polished faceted bead H
One 8mm blue scarab fire polished faceted bead J
One 8mm copper capri fire polished faceted bead K
Seven 4mm gilt jump rings
A reel of purple size D beading thread

Tools

A size 13 beading needle
A pair of scissors to trim the threads
A small amount of clear nail polish

*The finished length of this tassel is 24cm
including the hanging loop.
It measures 14.5cm below the hanging loop.*

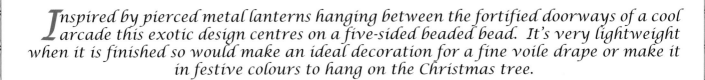

Inspired by pierced metal lanterns hanging between the fortified doorways of a cool arcade this exotic design centres on a five-sided beaded bead. It's very lightweight when it is finished so would make an ideal decoration for a fine voile drape or make it in festive colours to hang on the Christmas tree.

This Tassel is Made in Four Stages

A five-sided beaded bead is made in brick stitch - if you have not used brick stitch before please refer to page 10.

Five small tassels are assembled and attached to the corners of the beaded bead.

A separate large central tassel is prepared.

The whole design is brought together with the addition of the hanging loop.

1 The Five-Sided Beaded Bead - This starts with a foundation row which stretches around the equator of the beaded bead. Prepare the needle with 2m of single thread and tie a keeper bead 15cm from the end. Thread on 1D.

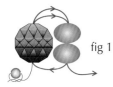 

fig 1   fig 2

2 Thread on 2A. Pass the needle through the D bead and the 2A in the same direction as before to bring the beads parallel to one another (fig 1). Thread on 3A. Pass the needle through the 2A of the previous stitch and back through the 3A of this stitch (fig 2) to complete the stitch.

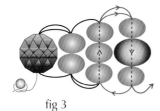

fig 3

3 Thread on 1A, 1B and 1A. Pass the needle through the 3A beads of the previous stitch and the three new beads (fig 3).

4 Referring to fig 4 thread on 1B, 1A and 1B. Pass the needle through the three beads of the previous stitch and the three beads of the new stitch.

Thread on 3B. Make the stitch as before.

Thread on 1B, 1E and 1B. Pass the needle through the 3B beads of the previous stitch and the new beads of this stitch (fig 4). This row will gape away from the previous row a little.

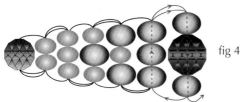

fig 4

Thread on 3B and make the stitch as before - as the previous row is over-length it will gape away from this row and will form a ridge that will stick out quite prominently from the stitches on either side.

5 Thread on 1B, 1A and 1B. Make the stitch as before. Make the following stitch with 1A, 1B and 1A.

Thread on 3A for the next stitch and make the final stitch with 2A (see fig 5).

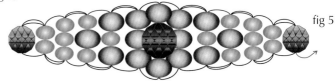

fig 5

Thread on 1D and stitch to the 2A of the previous row as before (fig 5).

6 Repeat Steps 2 to 5 inclusive three more times making sure that the ridge formed by the E beads always comes to the same side of the foundation row as the previous E bead.

Repeat Steps 2 to 5 once more finishing with 2A, to give a total of five repeats.

7 Bring the foundation row into a ring so that the first D bead comes up against the last stitch of 2A. Make sure that the ridges formed by the E beads are on the outside of the ring.

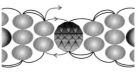

fig 6

Pass the needle down through the first D bead of the ring and back up through the 2A of the last stitch to join the two ends of the foundation row together (fig 6). Repeat the stitch to reinforce the join.

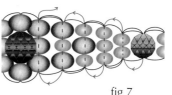

fig 7

Reposition the needle for the start of the next row by passing down and up through the previous four stitches to emerge through the top of the 3B stitch (fig 7).

The foundation ring will now support the brick stitch top and bottom of the beaded bead.

The ridges become the five corners of the bead.

Between the corners the brick stitch will form five triangular panels above and below the foundation row.

The shaping of the triangles is achieved by pinching in the overall bead shape at each corner and reducing the brick stitch count on two of the seven rows worked.

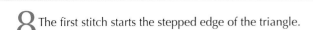

8 The first stitch starts the stepped edge of the triangle.

Thread on 2C. Pick up the second loop of thread along to the right of the bead that the thread has just emerged from (see fig 8). Pass the needle back up through the second of the 2C beads just added (fig 8) to bring the two new beads to sit parallel to one another on top of the foundation row.
A two-bead stitch is always used to start a row of brick stitch.

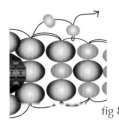
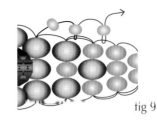

fig 8   fig 9

Thread on 1C. Pick up the next loop of thread along the foundation row and pass the needle back up through the new C bead (fig 9) bringing the new bead parallel to the previous C beads to complete a standard brick stitch.

Make seven more brick stitches in C to bring the needle to the first corner.

Extra Info....
The first two-bead stitch of the brick stitch row stretches the thread across the space for two and a half beads. This can cause the first bead to tip over slightly but it will stand up straight again when you finish the row and join the last bead to the first bead. Make sure that you pass the needle in the correct direction through the first bead when you make the join - follow the diagrams carefully.

9 You now need to reinforce the ridge on the foundation row formed by the E bead stitch.

Thread on 1D. Pick up the next TWO loops along the foundation row (one before the ridge and one after the ridge) by passing the needle across the corner formed by the ridge (fig 10).

Pass the needle back up through the D bead - you have now turned the corner.

top view

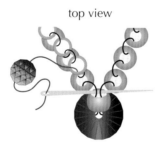

fig 10

10 Using C beads, work ten brick stitches to reach the next corner.

Repeat step 9 to turn the corner.

Repeat step 10 three more times.

To join the last D bead to the first C bead pass the needle down the first C bead, hook the needle underneath the loop of thread beneath it and pass back up through the first C bead (fig 11).

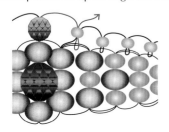

fig 11

11 Thread on 2C to start the new row. Make the stitch as before (fig 12).

Make two single stitches.

The next stitch needs to stretch across two loops to decrease the work above the D bead of the foundation row.

Thread on 1C and pick up the second loop along the top edge of the work.

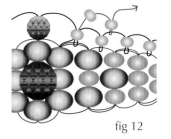

fig 12

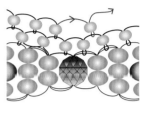

fig 13

Pass the needle back up the C bead just added to complete the decreasing stitch (fig 13).

Work three single C bead stitches to reach the corner (8C in total).

12 Make the corner stitch - thread on 1B and pass the needle under the next two loops (either side of the D bead from the previous row) (fig 14).

Pass the needle back up through the B bead so that it comes down to sit on top of the D bead from the previous row.

top view

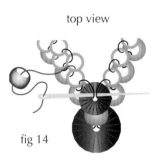

fig 14

Work four C bead brick stitches along the next four loops - the next stitch is the decreasing stitch. Work this stitch as in fig 13. Work three C brick stitches to the next corner.

Repeat step 12 three more times.

Join the last B bead of the row to the first C bead as fig 11.

13 The next row is worked without a decreasing stitch.

Start the row with a 2C stitch as fig 12. Work five single C bead stitches up to the next corner and repeat the B bead stitch as fig 14.

Work seven single C bead stitches to the next corner and repeat the B bead stitch. Repeat to work the three remaining sides and corners in a similar fashion. Link the last B bead to the first C bead of the row as fig 11.

14 Work the next row as for the previous row - you will find you have just six C beads between the B bead corners on this row. Link the last B bead of the row to the first C bead as before.

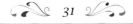

15 Work the first stitch of the next row with 2C beads as before. Make a decreasing stitch as fig 13 and work one single C bead stitch to make 4C beads in total. Turn the corner with 1B.
Work two single C bead stitches, a decreasing stitch and 1C. Turn the corner with 1B. Repeat to the end of the row. Join the last 1B bead of the row to the first C bead as before.

16 Work the next row without the decreasing stitch - you will have 3C beads between the B bead corners. Join the last B to the first C bead to complete.

Work the last row without the decreasing stitch - you will have just 2C beads between the B bead corners. Join the last B bead to the first C bead to complete. Leave the thread end loose and remove the needle.

Attach a new 1.2m length of single thread to the foundation row ready to work the other half of the bead. Make sure that the needle emerges from a 3B stitch immediately after an E bead stitch and begin with fig 8. When the beading is complete leave the thread end loose and remove the needle.

Set the beaded bead aside for the moment.

17 The Small Tassels - Before you start these tassels sort the fire polished faceted beads into three piles -

For the small tassels - 5D, 20E and 5F.
For the larger central tassel - 5D, 5G and 1H
For the main assembly - 1G, 1J and 1K.

Put aside the beads for the larger central tassel and the main assembly.

Prepare the needle with 1.5m of single thread and tie a jump ring 15cm from the end with a double knot - make sure that the thread does not pull through the gap in the ring.

Extra Info....
When using a jump ring to hold the threads at the top of a tassel there is a possibility of the threads slipping through the break in the ring. To prevent this dab the exposed threads with a little clear drying nail polish or glue - this will stick the threads to the ring and protect them from wear at the same time.

18 Thread on 1B, 1C, 1A, 1E, 1A, 1C, 1A, 1B, 1A, 1C, 1F, 1C, 1A, 1C and 1D.

* Thread on 7C, 2A, 1B, 1A 1E, 1A and 1C.

Turn the needle and pass it back up through the last A bead threaded to bring the last C bead up into an anchor for the strand (fig 15).

fig 15

Pass the needle back up through the remaining beads just added to emerge alongside the jump ring.

Pass the needle through the jump ring and down through the first fifteen beads to emerge from the D bead - this is where the remaining two tassel strands will hang from.

Working from * thread on the beads indicated for the strand, make the anchor as in fig 15 and pass the needle back up to the jump ring. Pass the needle through the jump ring and down through the first fifteen beads to emerge through the D bead once more.

Make the final strand of this tassel as for the previous strand, finishing with the needle emerging alongside the jump ring.

Tie the needle end of the thread securely to the other thread end with a double knot. Pass the needle down through the first few beads of the strand to neaten and trim close.

Attach the needle to the other thread end, neaten and trim this end in a similar fashion.

Make four more identical tassels and set them aside for the moment.

19 The Central Tassel - Prepare the needle with 1.5m of single thread and tie a jump ring 15cm from the end with a double knot - make sure that the thread does not pull through the gap in the ring.

Thread on 1H and push up to the jump ring. **Thread on 25C, 1A, 2C, 2A, 1C, 1B, 1C, 4A, 1B, 1C, 1D, 1C, 1B, 2A, 2C, 2A, 1C, 1A, 1B, 1C, 1G, 1C, 1B and 3C.

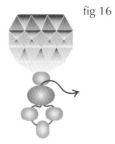

fig 16

Leaving aside the last 3C beads to anchor the strand pass the needle up through the last B bead threaded (fig 16) and all of the following beads to emerge from the top of the H bead adjacent to the jump ring.

Pass the needle through the jump ring and back down the H bead.

You are now in the correct position to begin the second strand of the tassel.

Repeat from ** four more times to make five tassel strands in total - finish with the needle emerging from the top of the H bead adjacent to the jump ring. Finish off the thread ends as for the small tassels.

20 Assembling the Tassel - Return to the longest thread end attached to the large beaded bead and attach the needle to this end.

Reposition the needle so that it emerges through one of the E beads on the ridges of the foundation row (fig 17).

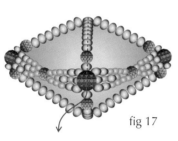

fig 17

fig 18

Pass the needle through the jump ring at the top of the first small tassel and back up through the E bead pulling the jump ring up close to the E bead (fig 18).

Pass the needle back up through the B and D beads of that corner of the beaded bead and down through the B and D beads of the next corner to emerge through the E bead at that corner (fig 19).

fig 19

The needle is now in the correct position to add the next small tassel to this corner of the beaded bead. Add the tassel to this corner and repeat to add the remaining three tassels to the other three corners of the beaded bead. Finish off the thread end neatly and securely.

21 Prepare the needle with 1.5m of double thread and tie a keeper bead 15cm from the end. Thread on 1J, 1C, 1B, 1C and 1G. Pass the needle down through the beaded bead so that the small tassels all dangle from below the E beads that they attach to. Thread on 1K and pass the needle through the jump ring at the top of the prepared central tassel. Turn the needle and pass it back up through the K bead, the beaded bead and the five beads above it to emerge alongside the keeper bead (fig 20).

Thread on 1C, 1A, 1B and 1A. The next beads make up the hanging loop. Thread on 14C, 1A, 1C, 3A, 1C, 1B, 1C, 3A, 1C, 1A, 24C, 1A, 1C, 3A, 1C, 1B, 1C, 3A, 1C, 1A, 4C and 1B. This is the midpoint of the hanging loop.

If you want to make the hanging loop any longer add more C beads now Finish any added C beads with 1B.

To complete the loop reverse the bead sequence starting with 4C, 1A, 1C, 3A, 1C and 1B etc.

fig 20

Pass the needle back down the A, B, A and C beads above the J bead to bring the needle out alongside the keeper bead. Remove the keeper bead and tie the two thread ends together securely.

Pass the thread ends through a few adjacent beads to neaten before trimming close.

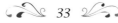

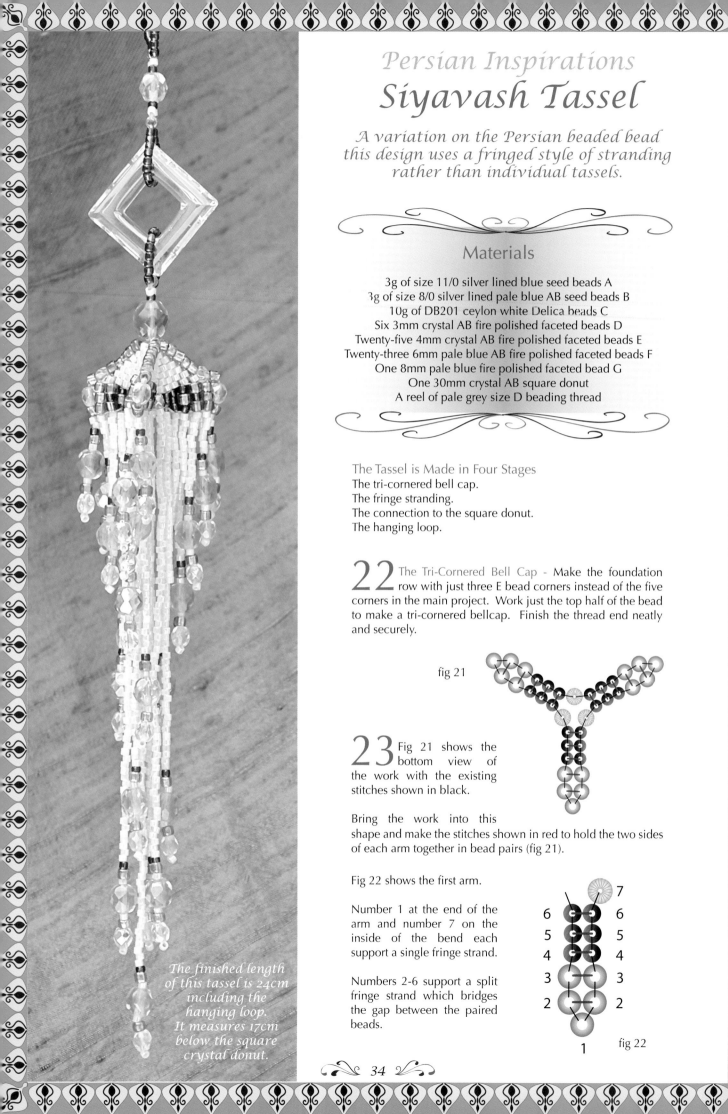

Siyavash Tassel

A variation on the Persian beaded bead this design uses a fringed style of stranding rather than individual tassels.

Materials

3g of size 11/0 silver lined blue seed beads A
3g of size 8/0 silver lined pale blue AB seed beads B
10g of DB201 ceylon white Delica beads C
Six 3mm crystal AB fire polished faceted beads D
Twenty-five 4mm crystal AB fire polished faceted beads E
Twenty-three 6mm pale blue AB fire polished faceted beads F
One 8mm pale blue fire polished faceted bead G
One 30mm crystal AB square donut
A reel of pale grey size D beading thread

The Tassel is Made in Four Stages
The tri-cornered bell cap.
The fringe stranding.
The connection to the square donut.
The hanging loop.

22 The Tri-Cornered Bell Cap - Make the foundation row with just three E bead corners instead of the five corners in the main project. Work just the top half of the bead to make a tri-cornered bellcap. Finish the thread end neatly and securely.

fig 21

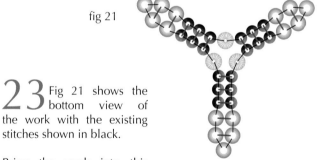

23 Fig 21 shows the bottom view of the work with the existing stitches shown in black.

Bring the work into this shape and make the stitches shown in red to hold the two sides of each arm together in bead pairs (fig 21).

Fig 22 shows the first arm.

Number 1 at the end of the arm and number 7 on the inside of the bend each support a single fringe strand.

Numbers 2-6 support a split fringe strand which bridges the gap between the paired beads.

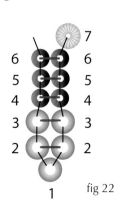

fig 22

The finished length of this tassel is 24cm including the hanging loop. It measures 17cm below the square crystal donut.

24 The Fringe Stranding - Attach a new 1.2m single thread to the work and pass the needle through the beads to emerge from bead number one at the tip of the first arm ready to make a fringe strand.

The bottom sequence for each strand is 1A, 1B, 1C, 1F, 1C, 1B, 1E and 1B (see figs 23 and 24).

For this first strand thread on 2C plus the bottom sequence as above (fig 23). Leave aside the last 1B to anchor the strand and pass back up through all of the beads added to emerge through bead 1 at the top.

Pass the needle down through one of the beads marked 2 on fig 22.

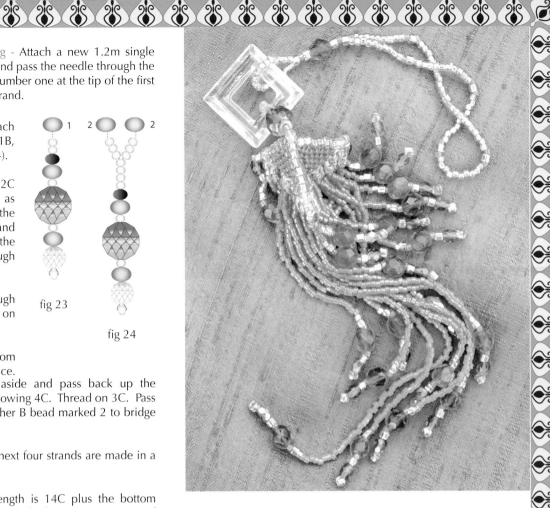

fig 23

fig 24

Make this fringe strand from 7C and the bottom sequence.
Leave the B anchor bead aside and pass back up the bottom sequence and the following 4C. Thread on 3C. Pass the needle up through the other B bead marked 2 to bridge across the gap (fig 24).

With reference to fig 22 the next four strands are made in a similar manner.

From bead 3 the strand length is 14C plus the bottom sequence. Pass back up through the bottom sequence and 8C. Add 6C and pass up into the other B bead marked 3 to bridge across the gap.

From bead 4 the strand length is 24C plus the bottom sequence. Pass back up through the bottom sequence and 13C. Add 11C and pass up into the other A bead marked 4 to bridge across the gap.

From bead 5 the strand length is 38C plus the bottom sequence. Pass back up through the bottom sequence and 20C. Add 18C and pass up into the other A bead marked 5 to bridge across the gap.

From bead 6 the strand length is 57C plus the bottom sequence. Pass back up through the bottom sequence and 30C. Add 27C and pass up into the other A bead marked 6 to bridge across the gap.

From bead 7 the strand is a single length with 72C above the bottom sequence.

Repeat the same sequence of strands all around the tri-cornered bead.

25 Suspend a final single strand, with 90C above the bottom sequence, from the central space by connecting to all three D beads to complete the fringe.

26 Connecting to the Square Donut - The G bead is connected to the top of the beaded cap by threads running up from the three B bead corners. Use a separate thread for each corner adding the G bead, 1A and 1B before creating a 17A loop to connect to the square donut. The three threads running through the loop will make it very strong.

27 The Hanging Loop - Prepare the needle with 1m of double thread. Tie a keeper bead 15cm from the end and thread on 1F, 1A, 1C, 1B and 1C.

Pass the needle back up the A and F beads to make a picot (fig 25). Thread on 1A, 1C, 1B and 1C. Pass back down the 1A bead just added and the F bead. Pass through the following 1C and 1B beads (fig 26).

Thread on 17A and pass the needle through the crystal donut.

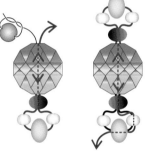

fig 25   fig 26

Pass the needle through the B bead on the tip of the picot in the same direction as before to pull up the loop (fig 27).

Pass the needle through the beads of the 17A loop once more to make it strong. Pass up through the remaining beads to emerge from the B bead at the other end of the F bead (fig 28).

fig 27   fig 28

Thread on sufficient A beads to make a suitable hanging loop. Pass the needle back through the B bead at this end of the F bead in the same direction as before to close up the loop.
Pass the needle through the beads of this loop again to make it strong. Finish off the remaining thread ends neatly and securely.

Turkish Knot Tassel

You Will Need

Materials

12g of size 10/0 bronze scarab seed beads A
4g of size 10/0 silver lined gold seed beads B
2.5g of size 3 silver lined gold bugle beads C
Two 12mm topaz fire polished faceted beads D
Five 6mm topaz fire polished faceted beads E
Twelve 3mm gilt metallic beads F
Six 6x4mm antique gold coloured corrugated metallic bicone beads G
One gilt 4mm jump ring
1m of stranded beading wire
Two gilt French crimps
A reel of black size D beading thread

Tools

A size 10 beading needle
A pair of scissors to trim the threads
A pair of flat-faced pliers for securing the crimps
Clear-drying nail polish to stiffen the main bead

*The finished length of this tassel is 26cm
including the hanging loop.
It measures 19cm below the hanging loop.*

*R*eminiscent of the elaborate turbans worn by the Djinn in the Tales of the Arabian Nights, the seed beads build up the hollow spiral beaded bead at the top of this lightweight tassel. The more elaborate Inspiration project is the Ottoman Tassel which would be perfect for Scheherazade's palace.

The Tassel is Made in Three Stages
The helix bead is constructed in circular peyote stitch.
The tassel strands are assembled onto a jump ring.
The helix bead and the tassel are drawn together and the hanging loop is added to the top.

Extra Info....
The helix bead pattern starts with the longest row around the centre of the bead and works up towards the top. The needle is then re-attached to the long row and worked down towards to the bottom to complete the shaping. Be careful not to pull the thread too hard on the first few rows or you may create a 'waist' around the centre of the beaded bead, however as you begin the decreasing stitches you will need to pull the thread a little tighter to define the spiral.

1 The Helix Bead - Prepare the needle with 3m of single thread. Tie a keeper bead 1.5m from the end (the long tail of thread will be used to complete the other half of the helix). Thread on 42A and 2B. Pass through all of the beads a second time to bring them into a circle (fig 1), emerging after the last B bead.

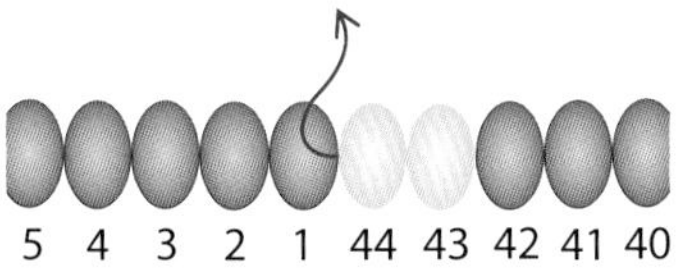

fig 1

5 4 3 2 1 44 43 42 41 40

fig 2

5 4 3 2 44 43 42 41 40
            1

fig 3

5 4 2 44 43 42 41
     3 1

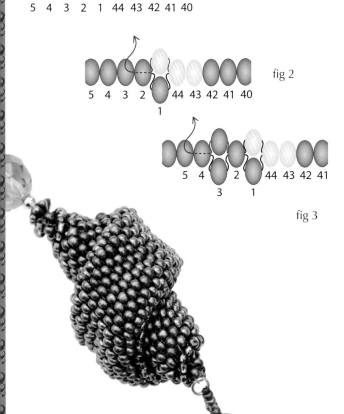

2 Thread on 1B and pass the needle through the second A bead along to bring the new bead to sit above the first A bead of the ring (fig 2). Thread on 1A and pass the needle through the fourth A bead of the first row (fig 3) pulling the new bead to sit above the third A bead of the first row.

Continue to add 1A at a time passing through alternate beads of the row adjusting the tension as you go to form a keyhole effect of two beads/one bead around the circle. Finish the row with the last new A bead pulling in above the first B bead and the needle passing through the last B bead of the first row (fig 4).

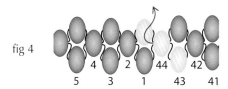

fig 4

4 2 44 42
5 3 1 43 41

This is the start of the peyote stitch technique.
You have created a circular row of keyholes for the next row of key beads to fit into. These key beads will, in turn, create the next row of keyholes.

Extra Info....
Wind the long tail of thread around a small piece of card to keep it tidy whilst you bead this part of the design.

3 You must now reposition the needle for the next row - this is called the 'step up'.

Pass the needle through the B bead directly above the first bead of row one (fig 5).

You are now in the correct position to add the first bead of this new row.

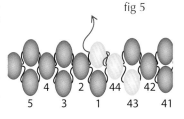

fig 5

4 2 44 42
5 3 1 43 41

Thread on 1B and pass the needle through the new key bead directly above the third bead of row one (fig 6). Continue to work around adding 1A to fill the keyholes between alternate beads.

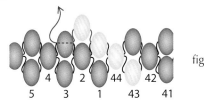

fig 6

4 2 44 42
5 3 1 43 41

4 Start the next row by 'stepping up' through the B bead at the start of the previous row. Thread on 1B for the first stitch of the new row (fig 7). Work the remainder of the row as before in A beads only.

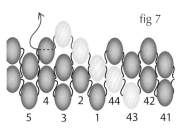

fig 7

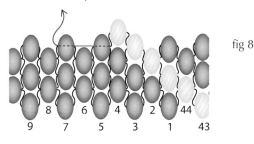

fig 8

5 Starting to decrease. Step up through the B bead at the start of the previous row. Make the first stitch as normal with 1B. Without adding a bead, stitch across the next keyhole to make the decrease (fig 8). Work the remainder of the row in A beads as before.

fig 9

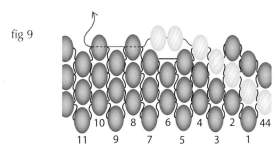

6 Next row - step up to the next row through the first B bead of the previous row as before. Thread on 2B and stitch across the decrease gap of the previous row. Without adding a bead, stitch across the next keyhole to decrease (fig 9). Work the remainder of the row in A beads as before.

7 Next row - Step up through the first 2B beads of the previous row. Add a 2B bead stitch across the decrease gap of the previous row and without adding a bead, stitch across the next keyhole to decrease (fig 10).

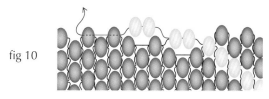

fig 10

Work the remainder of the row in A beads as before. The last A bead stitch will have to pass through the 2B beads above the first decrease.

Step up to the next row through the next 2B beads.

8 Thread on 2B beads and stitch across the last decrease gap and without adding a bead, stitch across the next keyhole (fig 11).

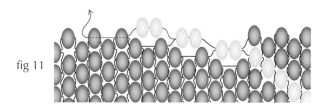

fig 11

Work the rest of the row in A beads as before until you get to the last stitch - thread on 1A and stitch across the first pair of B beads and through the following pair (fig 12) - this is the 'step up'.

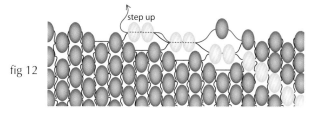

step up

fig 12

Repeat step 8 until the top of the spiral is reduced to five beads.

Pass the needle through these five beads a few times to strengthen the top of the work. Finish off the thread end neatly and securely.

9 Remove the keeper bead at the beginning of the work. Attach the needle to this end of the thread and you will be ready to work the other half of the bead. Step up through the 2B of the first row so that the first bead you add will be 1B.

Work from fig 6 in step 3 to the end of step 8 to complete this half of the bead.

To emphasise the spiral contour pass the needle through the last B bead in the opposite direction and all of the following B beads to emerge at the other end of the beaded bead. Pull the thread quite firmly as this will also help to stiffen the shape a little.

Finish off the thread end neatly and securely.

10
The Tassel - Prepare the needle with 2.5m of single thread. Tie a 4mm jump ring 15cm from the end of the thread with a double knot - take care that the thread does not slip through the gap in the jump ring - do not trim the tail of the thread.

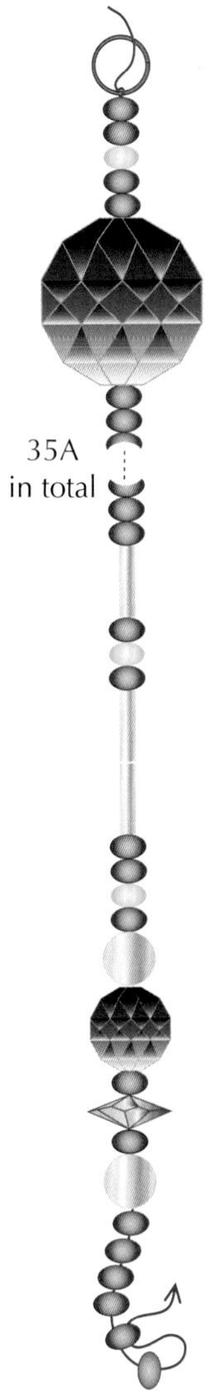

35A
in total

11
Sort through the A and B beads to find 4A and 1B beads with a slightly larger hole than the others.

Thread on these five beads in this order - 2A, 1B and 2A.

Now thread on 1D, 35A, 1C, 1A, 1B, 1A, 2C, 2A, 1B, 1A, 1F, 1E, 1A, 1G, 1A, 1F and 6A.

Leaving aside the last A bead threaded to anchor the strand, turn the needle and pass it back up through the fifth A of the last 6A beads just added (fig 13).

Thread on 3A. Pass the needle up through the A bead immediately below the F bead (fig 14).

Pass the needle through the following F bead and the remaining beads of the strand to emerge alongside the jump ring at the top of the strand.

fig 13

fig 14

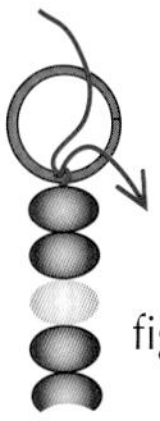

fig 15

Pass the needle through the jump ring (fig 15). Pass down the first five seed beads and the D bead to emerge immediately below the D bead - this is where you begin the next strand of the tassel.

12
Make the next strand as for the first but starting with 30A instead of 35A. Turn the needle at the top through the jump ring to emerge from the D bead ready to make the third strand.

Start the third strand with 25A. Work as before.

The fourth strand starts with 20A. Work as before.

The fifth strand starts with 15A. Work as before.

Pass the needle up to the jump ring for the final time and tie the needle end of the thread to the tail end of the thread firmly with a double knot. Pass both ends of the thread (one at a time) through the top few seed beads to conceal before trimming.

Paint the threads where they pass through the jump ring with a little nail polish or similar to protect them from wear.

Half of a helix bead makes a fabulous shell-shaped beaded bell cap or cone.

13
The Hanging Loop - Thread the jump ring at the top of the prepared tassel into the middle of the stranded beading wire. Bring the two ends of the wire together and pass up through the helix bead and 1G, 1F, 1D and 1F (fig 16).

14
Separate the wire ends and thread sufficient seed beads to make the hanging loop to your preferred length - you can use A beads, B beads or a combination of the two colours but do try to thread equal numbers onto both sides of the wire.

Thread two French crimps onto one end of the wire. Pass the other end of the wire in the opposite direction through the two crimps and pull the wire ends through to bring all of the beads up close to one another (fig 17).

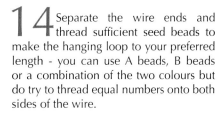

fig 16

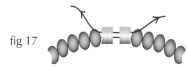

fig 17

Make sure you do not crush the helix bead with too much tension in the wire. Use your flat-faced pliers to squash the crimps completely flat which will grip the wire and secure the loop. Trim the wire ends very close to neaten.

15
The helix bead will need to be stiffened. Working in a well ventilated space manipulate the bead gently into its best shape and using clear nail polish paint the entire surface of the bead so that the varnish trickles down onto the threads between the beads. Hang up and leave to dry. Once dry give the bead a second coat and allow to dry thoroughly before handling.

Turkish Inspirations
Ottoman Tassel

Take the helix bead to jewelled heaven by adding a graduated fringe and encrusting embroidery. The decoration is topped off with a compound bead and a fancy hanging loop.

Materials

18g of size 10/0 garnet AB seed beads A
6g of size 10/0 silver lined gold seed beads B
6g of size 10/0 black seed beads C
4g of size 3 twisted black bugle beads D
Fifty-five 4mm garnet AB fire polished faceted beads E
Eighteen 6mm black fire polished faceted beads F
Thirty-three 5mm gilt filigree bead caps G
Seventeen 8mm gilt filigree bead caps H
Eighteen 3mm gold-coloured metallic round beads J
One 12mm black fire polished faceted bead K
1m of stranded beading wire
Two gilt French crimps
A reel of black size D beading thread

The finished length of this tassel is 31cm including the hanging loop.
It measures 26cm below the hanging loop.

This Tassel is Made in Four Stages
The helix bead.
The fringe strands.
The embellishment on the surface of the helix bead.
The hanging loop with the compound bead.

Follow steps 1 to 9 to complete the helix bead in the A and B beads.

16 The Fringe Strands - A fringe strand hangs from the bottom B bead of the helix and every second B bead up the helix until fifteen strands have been completed.

Attach a new thread to emerge through the bottom B bead of the helix with the needle pointing towards the next B bead along.

Thread on 56A, 1D, 1A, 1D, 4A, 1B, 4C, 1B, 1E, 1B, 1A and 1G to cup around 1F. Finish with 1J, 1A and 3C.

Leaving aside the last 3C bead to anchor the strand, pass the needle back up the last A bead and all of the following beads to emerge from the top of the strand.

Pass the needle through the B bead on the helix in the same direction as before and the following 2B (fig 18) ready to make the next strand.

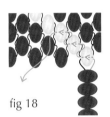

fig 18

17 Start the next strand with 45A instead of 56A. Make as for the first strand creating a 3C anchor at the bottom. Pass the needle through (as fig 18) to emerge from the second B bead up the helix at the top to be in the correct position to make the third strand.

The next eight strands follow the same lower sequence with a reduction in the number of A beads on each step.

Make the third strand with 36A at the top.
Make the fourth strand with 28A at the top.
Make the fifth strand with 22A at the top.
Make the sixth strand with 17A at the top.
Make the seventh strand with 13A at the top.
Make the eighth strand with 10A at the top.
Make the ninth strand with 7A at the top.
Make the tenth strand with 4A at the top.
The graduating sequence now removes the top D bead.

18 For the eleventh strand thread on 6A, 1D, 4A, 1B, 4C, 1B, 1E, 1B, 1A, 1G to cup around 1F, 1J, 1A and 3C. Complete the strand as before.

Make the twelfth strand with 1D, 4A, 1B, 4C, 1B, 1E, 1B, 1A, 1G to cup around 1F, 1J, 1A and 3C.
Make the thirteenth strand with 7A, 1B, 4C, 1B, 1E, 1B, 1A, 1G to cup around 1F, 1J, 1A and 3C.
Make the fourteenth strand with 5A, 1B, 4C, 1B, 1E, 1B, 1A, 1G to cup around 1F, 1J, 1A and 3C.
Make the fifteenth strand with 2A, 1B, 4C, 1B, 1E, 1B, 1A, 1G to cup around 1F, 1J, 1A and 3C. Finish off the thread end neatly and securely.

19 You now need to prepare a separate single fringe strand that will hang from the very bottom of the helix. Prepare the needle with 60cm of single thread and tie a keeper bead 10cm from the end.

Thread on 1E and 1A. Pass the needle back through the E bead to pull the A bead up close (fig 19).

fig 19

Thread on 65A, 1D, 1A, 1D, 4A, 1B, 4C, 1B, 1E, 1B, 1A, 1G to cup around 1F, 1J, 1A and 3C.

Make the anchor as before and pass the needle back up to emerge from the E bead at the top of the strand. Pass the needle through the single A bead and back down the E bead. Finish off the thread ends neatly and securely.

Set aside for the moment.

20 The Embellishment - This is stitched along the centre of the helical cushion. It starts 5mm past the draped position of the shortest fringe strand and works up to the top of the helix (see the main photo of the tassel). The needle will pass through the beads of the peyote-stitched surface quite easily - just weave through the bead holes one or two at a time.

The embellishing stitches place an E bead inside an H filigree cap.

When threading the bead sequences for the tassel stranding, the needle passed through the central threading hole on the G caps (hole X on fig 20). This brings the filigree cap to sit like a hat over the top of the bead.

fig 20

For the embellishment you need to create a different effect.

When making the embellishing stitches, the needle will pass from side to side through the filigee cap, holding a bead in the centre like a cup in a saucer. Referring to fig 20 the needle passes through one of the Z holes, one E bead and out of the cap through the opposite Z hole.

Note - the needle has to pass from the outside of the cap to the inside and then from the inside to the outside through these Z holes to pull the E bead into the centre of the saucer shape successfully.

21 Attach a new 1.5m single thread to the surface of the helix bead to emerge 5mm past the shortest fringe strand in the middle of the cushioned profile.

Pass the needle up through one of the Z holes on an H filigree cap; through 1E and down through the opposite Z hole on the cap (fig 21) to pull the E bead into the centre of the filigree cap.

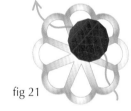

fig 21

Stitch through the A beads of the helix to secure the cap to the surface of the beadwork. Work the needle through the A beads to emerge 6mm further along the helix cushion. Add a second cap with an E bead centre - the edge of this cap should sit 3mm from the edge of the previous cap.

Continue up the centre of the helical cushion adding a further twelve E bead and H filigree cap combinations.

The available cushion will now be starting to reduce in width - you may have room for one or two more H caps but then you will need to swap to the G caps. You may fit four or five of the G caps (with an E bead centre) along the cushion before it peters out at the top. Leave the thread end attached and remove the needle.

22 Each cap is now enhanced with a collar of C beads. Add a new 1.2m single thread to emerge alongside the first H cap.

Thread on 17C. Drape the C beads around the underside of the first cap to form a tight-fitting circle (fig 22).

fig 22

Pass the needle through the beads a second time to secure the circle. Fix the circle to the A beads of the helix with two or three small stitches.

Pass the needle through the beads of the circle to emerge from one of the C beads between this cap and the next cap along. You need to make a circle to surround the second cup that will link to the first circle.

fig 23   fig 24

Look at your work - in fig 23 the two caps have 3C beads between them so the two circles will share 3C - your circle may be slightly different. Pass the needle through to the last of these C beads to share and thread on 14C beads to complete a 17C circle around the next cap (fig 24). Secure this circle with a few stitches to the A beads of the helix and move onto the next cap. Repeat around all of the H caps.

Stitch 2C or 3C beads between the edges of the G caps as there will not be sufficient space for anything further.

Finish off the thread ends neatly and securely.

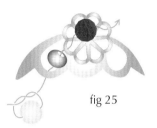

23

The Compound Bead & Final Assembly - You need to start by making the compound bead. This will encase the K bead in a cage of bead caps, C and E beads.

Referring to fig 20 the needle will pass through the Z holes in the caps from the outside to the inside of the cap and then from the inside to the outside.

First you will decorate 2H caps. Prepare the needle with 60cm of single thread and tie a keeper bead 10cm from the end. Pass from the inside to the outside of 1H through a Z hole and thread on 1C.

fig 25

*Thread on 1G from the outside to the inside through a Z hole. Thread on 1E.

Pass the needle from the inside to the outside of the same G cap through the opposite Z hole (fig 25).

Thread on 1C.

Locate the second Z hole around the H cap and pass the needle from the outside to the inside of the cap.

fig 26

Pass the needle in the opposite direction through the next Z hole and through the C bead (fig 26) to pull the small cap firmly into place, so the C bead sits on top of the divider between these Z holes.

Repeat from * once.

Thread on 1G with an E bead centre. Pass the needle through the first C bead of the decoration and the next Z hole of the H cap around to make this C bead straddle the ribs of the cap as before.

Remove the keeper bead and tie the two ends of the thread together tightly inside the H cap.

Seal with a dab of clear nail polish or glue and trim the ends close.

24

Repeat to make a second decorated H cap - this time start with 80cm of thread and do not trim the needle thread away after you make the knot.

The compound beads made into lantern shaped earrings.

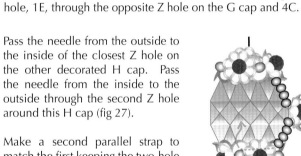

25

Pass the needle to the outside of the second decorated H cap through one of the Z holes. Position the decorated H caps onto each end of the K Bead. Pass the end of the stranded beading wire from top to bottom of this arrangement to keep the three elements in line as you work.

There are eight Z holes in each of the H caps - you will need to make four straps between the two H caps to encase the K bead.

Thread on 4C, 1G from the outside to the inside through a Z hole, 1E, through the opposite Z hole on the G cap and 4C.

Pass the needle from the outside to the inside of the closest Z hole on the other decorated H cap. Pass the needle from the inside to the outside through the second Z hole around this H cap (fig 27).

Make a second parallel strap to match the first keeping the two-hole spacing on the caps.

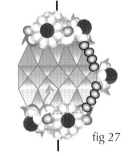

fig 27

Repeat to complete four straps in total pulling firmly on the thread to bring the decorated H caps up close to the K bead.

Finish off the thread end neatly and securely and remove the wire.

26

The Hanging Loop - Thread the 1A bead at the top of the single fringe strand made in step 19 into the middle of the stranded beading wire.

Pass both ends of the wire through the helix bead and 1B, 1E, 1J, 1F, 1G to cover the top of the F bead, 3C, the compound bead, 2C, 1G to cup over the preceding C beads, 1F, 1J, 1E and 1C. Separate the two strands to make the hanging loop.

The hanging loop is made from a combination of 1B, 1C, 1E, 1C and 1B separated by blocks of plain A beads. Thread up the loop to the desired length and secure with the crimps as in step 14.

Helter Skelter Tassel

You Will Need

Materials

4g of size 8/0 blue scarab seed beads A
7g of size 10/0 frost silver lined blue AB seed beads B
5g of size 10/0 silver lined turquoise seed beads C
3g of size 10/0 ceylon white seed beads D
2g of size 10/0 silver lined crystal seed beads E
3g of size 3 twisted blue scarab bugle beads F
Thirty-five 4mm crystal AB fire polished faceted beads G
Eighteen 6mm turquoise AB fire polished faceted beads H
Thirteen 4mm blue fire polished faceted beads J
A reel of white size D beading thread

Tools

A size 10 beading needle
A pair of scissors to trim the threads

*The finished length of this tassel is 22cm
including the hanging loop.
It measures 18cm below the hanging loop.*

*U*nlike many of the other tassels in this collection, this elegant spiral is made around a flexible core and not suspended from a head bead or decorative motif. A sinuous design that would make a fabulous tassel decoration for an evening bag or, perhaps made a little smaller, on the ends of a Twenties-style lariat necklace.

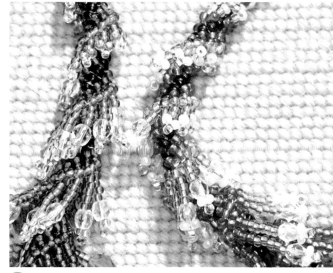

This Tassel is Made in Four Stages
The main stranding is made around a spiral rope core.
An additional set of three strands is added to the bottom.
The spirals are brought into a continuous line.
The hanging loop is added to the top.

1 The Spiral Stranding - The stranding is supported on a spiral rope base where a plain core is overlaid with a series of more detailed sequences. Starting at the top, the rope begins with a few simple repeats. The outer sequence of each stitch then starts to introduce the tassel strands.

Unusually the tassel is worked upside-down with the tassel strands pointing away from you as you work. This enables the needle to pass through the beads at the centre of the rope more easily and keeps the developing tassel strands out of the way a little more.

Extra Info....
The diagrams and instructions show the last row on each step of the rope being pushed to the left to form the spiral. This is ideal if you are right-handed as it creates more room for the needle to the right. If you are left-handed push the last row to the right to give yourself an equal amount of access.

2 Prepare the needle with 2m of single thread and tie a keeper bead 25cm from the end. Thread on 4A, 1B, 1C, 1D, 1C and 1B. Pass the needle through the 4A beads to bring the five smaller beads into a strap to the side (fig 1). Push the smaller beads to the left as seen in fig 1.

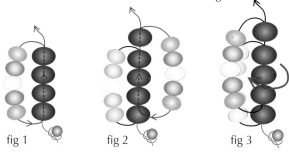

fig 1   fig 2   fig 3

Thread on 1A, 1B, 1C, 1D, 1C and 1B. Pass the needle through the last 3A of the previous stitch and the new 1A to bring the five smaller beads into a strap to the side (fig 2). Push the new stitch to the left (fig 3).

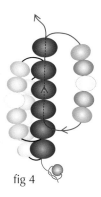

fig 4

This is a simple spiral rope. On each stitch you add one bead to the core (1A) and a combination of beads to make the outer pattern. The needle passes up through the last three core beads of the previous stitch and the new core bead (four core beads in total).

For the next stitch thread on 1A, 1B, 1C, 1D, 1C and 1B. Pass the needle through the last 3A of the previous stitch and the new 1A (fig 4). Push the new stitch to the left as in fig 3.

3 Make one more stitch as in fig 4 pushing the completed stitch to the left where you should be able to see the spiral beginning to form.

The tassel stranding now starts with a very small picot decoration. Each tassel strand is attached to the middle bead of the five size 10/0 seed beads that makes up each rope stitch. After the 1A for the core you add the first three of these five beads, make the tassel strand and then add the final two beads completing the stitch as before by passing through the core.

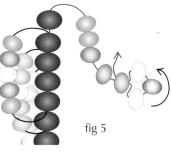

fig 5

4 Thread on 1A, 2B, 3C, 1D, 1E and 1D. Push these beads down to the core.

Pass the needle through the last C bead threaded in the opposite direction to draw the last three beads into a picot (fig 5).

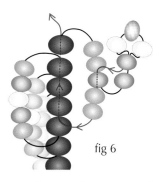

fig 6

Referring to fig 6 pass the needle through the first C bead of this step in the same direction as before and thread on 2B. Pass the needle through the four core beads as before (fig 6).

If necessary adjust the tension in the thread so the first 2C beads of this step sit parallel to one another as shown in fig 6. You will notice that the picot has flipped to point away from you. Push the stitch to the left.

Repeat step 4 five times to give six repeats in total - make sure to push each stitch to the left before you start the next repeat. Adjust the tension on each stitch so that the picot points away from you as in fig 6.

For clarity the following diagrams will show the stitch being worked and the previous completed stitch only.

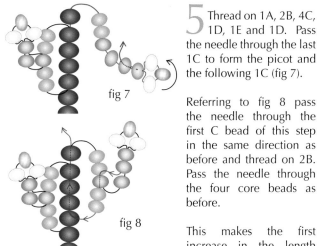

fig 7

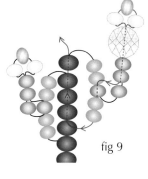

fig 8

5 Thread on 1A, 2B, 4C, 1D, 1E and 1D. Pass the needle through the last 1C to form the picot and the following 1C (fig 7).

Referring to fig 8 pass the needle through the first C bead of this step in the same direction as before and thread on 2B. Pass the needle through the four core beads as before.

This makes the first increase in the length of the tassel strand.

Make sure the tension is correct in the strand so the first 2C beads are sitting parallel to one another as before. Push the stitch to the left.

Repeat this stitch four times to give you five repeats in total.

6 The next increase adds a G bead to the strand length. Thread on 1A, 2B, 4C, 1G, 1D, 1E and 1D.

Referring to fig 9 pass the needle through the G bead to form the picot and the following 2C. Pass the needle through the first C bead of this step in the same direction as before and thread on 2B. Pass the needle through the four core beads (fig 9). Check the tension in the strand and push the stitch to the left.

fig 9

Repeat this stitch four times to give you five repeats in total.

7 The strand length now starts to increase between the G bead picot and the two parallel beads at the top of the strand. The thread path stays the same at the picot and at the two parallel beads.

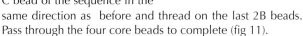

Referring to fig 10 thread on 1A, 2B, 5C, 1G, 1D, 1E and 1D.

Make the picot at the end as before and pass back through the 3C following the G bead as shown.

Pass the needle through the first C bead of this step in the same direction as before and thread on 2B. Pass the needle through the four core beads (fig 10).

fig 10

Repeat this stitch two more times.

The next sequence increases the strand length by 1C so this time you need to thread on 1A, 2B, 6C, 1G, 1D, 1E and 1D.

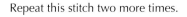

Following fig 11 you can see the thread path is the same as before. Make the picot first and pass back through 4C beads (as the strand is 1C longer). Pass through the first C bead of the sequence in the same direction as before and thread on the last 2B beads. Pass through the four core beads to complete (fig 11).

fig 11

Repeat this stitch two more times.

Following the same thread paths at the picot and the parallel beads you will need to make the next strand increase. Make three more stitches starting with 1A, 2B, 7C, 1G, 1D, 1E and 1D. This bead count will increase the strand length by a further 1C bead. Add 2B beads and pass through the four core beads to complete the stitch.

Repeat this stitch two more times.

8 The B bead is now blended into the top of the strand.

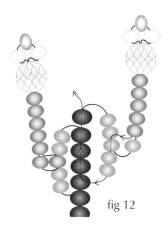

Referring to fig 12 thread on 1A, 4B, 5C, 1G, 1D, 1E and 1D.

Make the picot as before and pass the needle back through the following 5C beads.

fig 12

Pass the needle through the third B bead of this step in the same direction as before and thread on 2B. Pass the needle through the four core beads (fig 12).

The following steps will give the bead count for the first part of the stitch only - to complete each stitch you will have to add the last 2B beads of the spiral stitch and pass through the four core beads as on all of the previous tassel strands.

9 Make the next stitch with 1A, 5B, 5C, 1G, 1D, 1E and 1D which will increase the strand length by 1B bead (fig 13).

Make the next stitch with 1A, 6B, 5C, 1G, 1D, 1E and 1D which will increase the strand length by 1B bead.

Make the next stitch with 1A, 7B, 5C, 1G, 1D, 1E and 1D which will increase the strand length by 1B bead.

fig 13

You now have eighteen strands with a G bead above the picot.

In the next strand you will introduce an H bead.

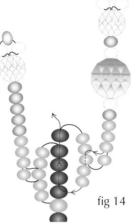

10 Make the next stitch with 1A, 7B, 1C, 1D, 1H, 1D, 1C, 1G, 1D, 1E and 1D (fig 14).

Increase the B bead count on the next three stitches to 9B, 11B and 13B.

You have completed four strands with a G and a H bead. In the next strand you will introduce a J bead.

fig 14

11 For the next stitch thread on 1A, 10B, 1C, 1J, 1C, 1B, 1C, 1D, 1H, 1D, 1C, 1G, 1D, 1E and 1D.
For the following stitch increase the count of 10B to 12B.

In the next strand you will introduce an F bead.

For the next stitch thread on 1A, 10B, 1F, 1B, 1C, 1J, 1C, 1B, 1C, 1D, 1H, 1D, 1C, 1G, 1D, 1E and 1D.
Increase the B bead count on the next four stitches to 13B, 16B, 18B and 20B.

The strand is now long enough to add the final F bead of the sequence.

Make the next stitch with 1A, 19B, 1F, 1C, 1B, 1C, 1F, 1B, 1C, 1J, 1C, 1B, 1C, 1D, 1H, 1D, 1C, 1G, 1D, 1E and 1D.
Make two more stitches - on the first increase the B bead count to 21B and on the last stitch to 23B.

12 The Three Strand Tassel - These three strands hang from the bottom of the spiral core.

The needle will be emerging from the bottom bead of the core. Thread on 1A, 19B, 1F, 1C, 1B, 1C, 1F, 1B, 1C, 1J, 1C, 1B, 1C, 1D, 1H, 1D, 1C, 1G, 1D, 1E and 1D. Make the picot at the end of the strand as before and pass back through the strand beads to emerge from the 1A bead just added.

Pass the needle through the bottom A bead of the core (fig 15).

fig 15

13 Pass the needle through the A bead just added to emerge at the top of the new tassel strand making a strap of thread over the outside of the last A bead of the core (fig 16).

For the next strand thread on 22B, 1F, 1C, 1B, 1C, 1F, 1B, 1C, 1J, 1C, 1B, 1C, 1D, 1H, 1D, 1C, 1G, 1D, 1E and 1D.

fig 16

Make the picot at the end of this strand as before and pass back through the strand beads to emerge from the A bead at the bottom of the core (as fig 15).

Reposition the needle again as in fig 16 for the last strand. Make the final strand from 25B, 1F, 1C, 1B, 1C, 1F, 1B, 1C, 1J, 1C, 1B, 1C, 1D, 1H, 1D, 1C, 1G, 1D, 1E and 1D.

14 Locate the last spiral stitch around the core.

Following fig 17 reposition the needle to emerge through the B bead sitting on top of the strand - note that the needle is pointing away from the strand.

Turn the tassel up the right way so all the strands fall naturally into place.

fig 17

Remove the needle but do not tie or trim the thread.

15 Before you move on you need to taper the top of the tassel a little.

Remove the keeper bead added in step 2 and attach the needle to this end (fig 18).

Thread on 1C, 1D, 1C and 1B.

fig 18

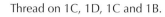

Pass the needle through the top 3A beads of the core (fig 19). Push this stitch to sit next to the last spiral stitch.

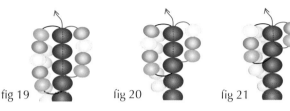

fig 19   fig 20   fig 21

Thread on 1D, 1C and 1B. Pass the needle through the top 2A beads of the core (fig 20) and push this stitch to sit alongside the previous stitch.

Thread on 1C and 1B. Pass the needle through the top A bead of the core (fig 21). Leave the thread end loose and remove the needle.

Reattach the needle to the thread end left loose at the end of step 14.

fig 22

16 Making a Continuous Line
To define the spiral the tops of all of the strands are linked together.

The needle has to pass through the single bead at the top of each strand - these beads are sitting parallel to the middle bead of the spiral stitch (see figs 6 to 14). The needle is currently emerging through the first bead of the sequence.

Fig 22 shows the beads at the top of the strands in orange. You will need to add a B or C bead between each strand - these are shown in green.

Thread on 1B and pass through the next strand top B bead in the direction shown in fig 22.

Repeat to make a link to the next strand top B bead (fig 22).

Repeat until the next top strand bead in the sequence is 1C.

Swap the spacing beads from B to C and continue to the top of the spiral.

Tension the thread so the spiral is well-defined but not so tight as to make the work stiff.

17 The Hanging Loop - Pass the needle through the beads at the top of the spiral to emerge through the top A bead of the core. Thread on 1H, and sufficient B, C, D and E beads to make a hanging loop of the desired length.

Pass the needle back down the H bead and through the two beads added in fig 21. Pass the needle up through the top A core bead, the H bead and the loop beads again to strengthen. Repeat once more.

Finish off all the remaining thread ends neatly and securely.

Helter Skelter Inspirations
Fairground Tieback

Why have just one tassel when you can have two?

Here the Helter Skelter Tassel is developed into a stylish curtain tieback with the spiral rope extending into a functional cord.

The longest tassel strand in this design hangs 25cm below the beaded bead.

The rope strap is 37cm long including the loops at the ends.

You Will Need

Materials

30g of size 8/0 frost silver lined gold seed beads A
50g of size 10/0 silver lined lime seed beads B
25g of size 10/0 silver lined eau de nil seed beads C
18g of size 10/0 silver lined grey seed beads D
12g of size 3 silver lined grey bugle beads F
Ninety-four 4mm olive AB fire polished faceted beads G
Thirty-eight 6mm grey AB fire polished faceted beads H
Forty-four 4mm topaz AB fire polished faceted beads J
A reel of ash size D beading thread

The Tieback is Made in Five Stages
The first tassel.
The rope extending to the second tassel.
The second tassel.
The spiral rope cord for the tieback itself.
The beaded tube at the centre.

Fig 23 gives you a skeleton
view of the tieback -
The tassels dangle from either
end of one rope.
The tieback rope has a loop at either
end to slip over a hook.
The beaded tube conceals the join between
the two ropes.

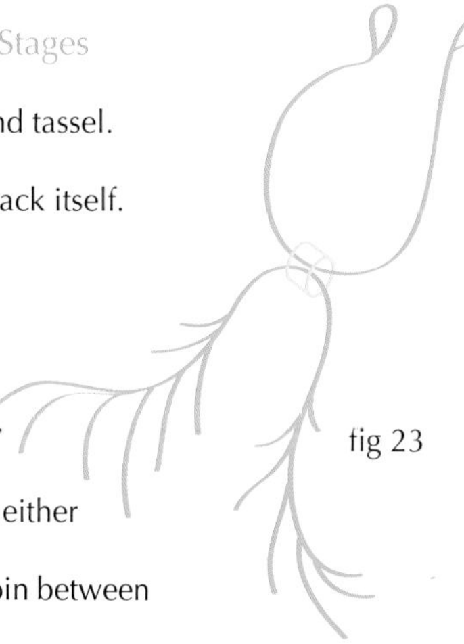

fig 23

18 The First Tassel - Following steps 1 to 14 inclusive make a tassel. Note there is no E bead - use the C beads as a substitute where necessary. Leave the thread end loose at the bottom of the tassel.

19 The Connecting Rope - Return to the top of the tassel and attach a 1.5m single thread length passing the needle through to emerge from the top A bead of the core.

Following figs 2, 3 and 4 resume the spiral rope at the top of the work. Work the rope to measure 14cm from the top of the first tassel.

20 The Second Tassel - Repeat steps 4 to 14 inclusive to make a second tassel.

21 Following step 16 link the top of all of the strands on this second tassel together. Stop when you pass through the top C bead of the first picot strand on this tassel.

The middle D beads of the spiral rope between the two tassels are now linked together with a continuation of the same thread.

Fig 24 shows the top picot strand of the tassel to the bottom left - the needle should be emerging from the top bead of this strand. Thread on 1C (shown in purple in fig 24) and pass up through the D bead in the middle of the next spiral stitch (see fig 24).

fig 24

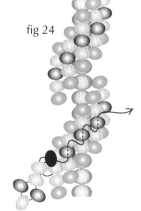

Pass the needle up through the D bead at the centre of the next two spiral stitches (fig 24).

Repeat all the way along the rope until you reach the top picot on the first spiral.

Work down the top tassel strand beads on this tassel adding in the appropriate spacer beads as in step 16.

Finish off all the remaining thread ends neatly and securely. The spiral rope will feel more firm and the spiralling pattern of the toning beads will be more pronounced.

22 The Spiral Rope Cord - Prepare the needle and start a rope as in step 2. Work the same repeat until the rope is 25cm long. You may want to make a longer cord - if you do, add the extra stitches now. The looped ends made in the next step will add 40mm to each end of the rope.

23 Thread on 1H, 1A and twelve repeats of 1G, 1A. Pass the needle through the first 1A and the following 1H to draw up the loop and emerge at the end of the rope.

Pass the needle through the five outer beads of the last spiral stitch and back through the last four core beads (fig 25).

fig 25

Pass the needle through the H bead, the following 1A and the beads of the loop. Pass back through the first A bead and the H bead again. Turn the needle through the beads of the rope as fig 25 and repeat to strengthen the loop.

If the needle will fit through the beads a fourth time repeat again to make the loop as strong as possible.

24 Referring to fig 24 pass the needle through the D beads along the length of the spiral rope cord to bring continuity to the spiral and the needle through to the other end of the rope.

Reposition the needle to emerge from the end A bead of the core and make a bead loop as in step 23.

Bring the two spiral ropes together. The tasselled length needs to link to the middle of the looped length but the tassels need to be slightly offset so they hang at different heights.

Decide on your preferred arrangement and make a few simple stitches between the two ropes where they touch (fig 26).

The beaded tube will conceal the linkage.

fig 26

25 The Beaded Tube - Prepare a 1.2m single thread with a keeper bead 15cm from the end. Thread on 1B, 1F, 2B, 1F and 1B. Pass the needle up through the first three beads and down through the second to make an oblong (fig 27). This is ladder stitch.

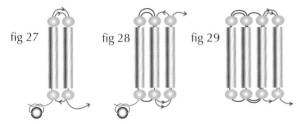

fig 27   fig 28   fig 29

Thread on 1B, 1F and 1B. Pass the needle down through the previous three beads to bring the new beads up parallel. Pass the needle up through the new beads (fig 28).

Thread on 1B, 1F and 1B and repeat to give you 4F in a row with B bead rocailles at either end of each bugle bead (fig 29).

Repeat until you have 18F in a row.

26 Wrap the ladder around the link between the two spiral ropes. Join the two ends of the ladder together with two firm stitches (fig 30).

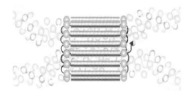

fig 30

27 The needle will be emerging from a B bead on the edge of the tube. Thread on 1J and 1D. Pass the needle back through the J bead and the 1B, 1F and 1B beads below it (fig 31).

fig 31

fig 32

Thread on 1J and 1D.

Pass the needle back through the J bead and the following 1B, 1F and 1B beads.

Pass down the next 1B, 1F and 1B and up the next three beads (fig 32).

28 Repeat step 27 until you have 9J beads around each edge of the tube.

Pass the needle through the work to emerge from the closest D bead at the top of a J bead.

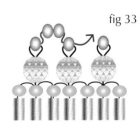

fig 33

Thread on 2D and pass through the next 1D along (fig 33).

Repeat until you have completed a collar of D beads around this end of the tube. Repeat at the other end of the tube to match.

Finish off all of the remaining thread ends neatly and securely.

Heligan Tassel

You Will Need

Materials

10g of size 10/0 pink lined pale topaz seed beads A
4g of size 10/0 silver lined dark gold seed beads B
4g of size 8/0 silver lined frost grey AB seed beads C
14g of size 10/0 green lined pale topaz seed beads D
4g of size 3 silver lined dark gold bugle beads E
Seventeen 4mm topaz AB fire polished faceted beads F
Twelve 8x6mm bronze metallic oval crystal beads G
Twenty-eight 8x6mm green AB oval crystal beads H
Three 6x4mm metallic bronze crystal rondelles J
Seven 6x4mm amethyst crystal rondelles K
One 8x6mm amethyst crystal rondelle L
One 18mm tequilla sunrise cushioned crystal disc M
A reel of ash size D beading thread

Tools

A size 10 beading needle
A pair of scissors to trim the threads

The finished length of this tassel is 25cm
including the hanging loop.
It measures 20cm below the hanging loop.

*F*ind a quiet corner in a summertime English garden & your senses are overloaded with vibrant colours, heady scents & the hum of busy insects. The soft pinks & gold in this design are reminiscent of a glorious Rudbeckia, but made in icy white & silver transforms it into a fabulous winter decoration to hang on your Christmas tree.

This Tassel is Made in Three Stages

The flower motif is created around the crystal M bead.
The fringe stranding is added to the lower points.
The hanging loop is worked from the top of the flower.

1 The Crystal Flower - Prepare the needle with 2m of single thread and tie a keeper bead 15cm from the end.

Thread on 1M, 1A, 1F, 1A, 1F, 1A, 1F, 1A, 1F, 1A, 1F and 1A. Pass the needle through the M bead in the same direction as before to bring the A and F beads into a strap around the side of the M bead (fig 1).

fig 1

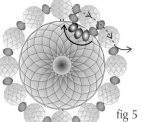

fig 2

2 Thread on 1A, 1F, 1A, 1F, 1A, 1F, 1A, 1F, 1A, 1F and 1A.

Pass the needle through the M bead in the same direction as before to bring the A and F beads into a strap around the other side of the M bead (fig 2).

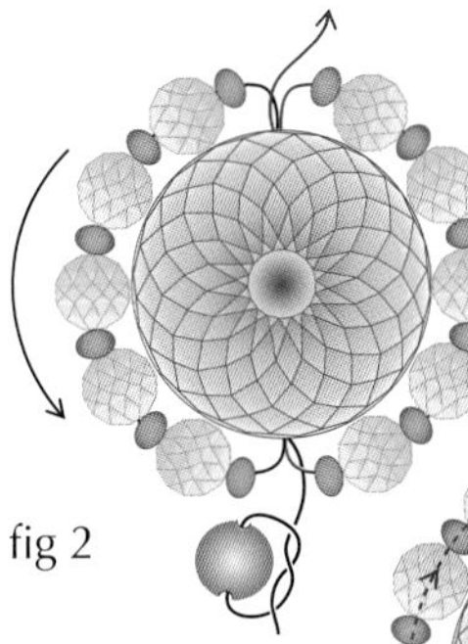

3 Pass the needle through the eleven A and F beads of the first stitch from step 1 and thread on 1F.

fig 3

Pass the needle through the eleven A and F beads added in step 2 to bring the new F bead to sit above the hole in the M bead (fig 3).

Thread on 1F and pass through the first 1A and 1F of the first stitch again to draw this F bead into position above the hole in the M bead (fig 4) and to complete a circular frame of A and F beads around the M bead.

fig 4

4 Thread on 1A, 3B and 1A. Pass the needle through the initial F bead in the same direction as before and the following 1A and 1F (fig 5).

fig 5

Following fig 6 thread on 1A and 3B. Pass the needle through the first A bead of the previous stitch and the following 1F, 1A and 1F of the circle (fig 6).

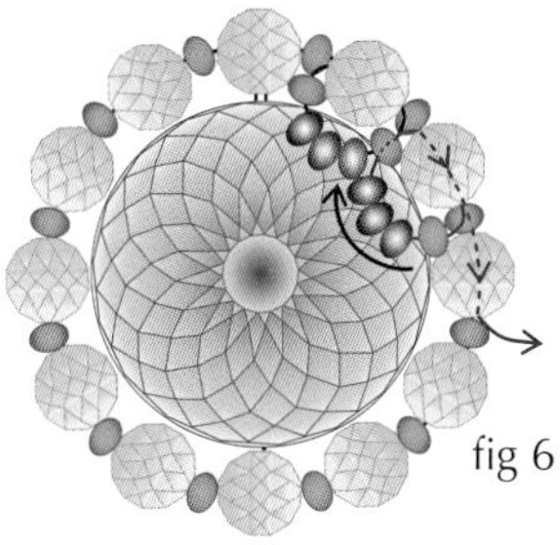

fig 6

Repeat this stitch nine more times, working around the circle, to emerge from the last F bead added in step 3.

5 To make the last stitch pass the needle through the adjacent A bead from the first stitch made in step 4 and thread on 3B.

Pass the needle through the first A bead of the previous stitch and the F bead once more (fig 7).

fig 7

fig 8

6 Reposition the needle passing through the adjacent A bead from the stitch made in step 4 and the following 3B of the first B bead stitch.

Following fig 8 pass the needle through the B beads to draw them into a complete circle. Finish with the needle emerging from the last B bead of the first 3B bead stitch (fig 8).

This has completed an inner rim for the A and F bead circular frame on this side of the work. You now need to work an identical rim on the other side of the M bead.

7 Pass the needle through the adjacent 1A and the following F bead. Flip the work over so you can see the other side of the M bead.

Repeat steps 4, 5 and 6 to complete an inner rim on this side of the work.

As before, pass the needle through the following 1A and the adjacent F bead to emerge at the outer edge of the frame ready to add the petal beads.

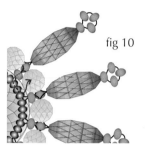

fig 9

8 The needle is emerging from an F bead. Thread on 1G and 4A.

Leaving aside the last 3A beads to form a picot pass the needle through the first A bead in the opposite direction and the following G bead (see fig 9).

Pass the needle through the following 1F of the frame around the M bead (fig 9).

Repeat step 8 eleven more times to add twelve G beads in total.

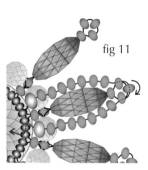

fig 10

9 Reposition the needle passing through the adjacent 1A bead of the rim and the following 2B below it on the rim (fig 10). The needle will be emerging from the B bead midway between the last A bead passed through and the next A bead of the rim.

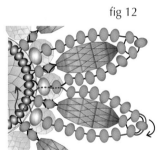

fig 11

Thread on 1C and 7A. Pass the needle through the 3A beads of the picot at the tip of the adjacent G bead (see fig 11).

Thread on 7A and 1C. Pass the needle through the B bead on the rim midway between the next 2A beads around the frame (fig 11).

Before moving on check the shape of the A bead frame around the G bead. The A beads should all sit snugly together leaving the 3A bead picot to form a point. Adjust the tension in the thread if necessary so the G bead is not pulled out of line and the picot is centralised and pointed.

fig 12

10 Referring to fig 12 pass the needle up through the last 1C and 1A beads added and thread on 6A.

Pass the needle through the 3A beads of the picot at the tip of the next G bead and thread on 7A and 1C.

Pass the needle through the B bead midway between the next 2A beads around the frame.

11 Repeat step 10 nine times to complete eleven petals. The twelfth petal needs to link the first petal. Make as for the previous ten petals but thread on just 6A after passing through the picot at the tip of the G bead. Pass down through the first 1A and 1C beads of the first petal and through the B bead on the rim as before. Pass the needle through the B beads of the rim to bring them into a neat alignment once more.

Pass the needle though the B, A and F beads of the rim and the circular frame to emerge from the B bead rim on the other side of the M bead. Make sure that the needle is positioned as in fig 10 ready to make the first petal frame on this side of the flower.

Repeat steps 9 and 10 to complete the petal frames on this side of the M bead and finish off the thread ends neatly and securely.

Note - for clarity the following diagrams will show just one layer of A beads around the G bead petals.

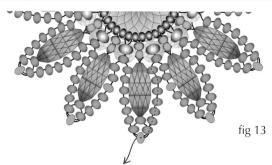

fig 13

12 The Fringe Strands - Fig 13 shows in blue the beads to which the fringe strands will attach. Five of the strands hang from the tips of the picots. The remaining two strands hang from A beads on the sides of the petal frames - these two strands are suspended between the corresponding A beads on both the front and the back of the flower.

Prepare the needle with 1.5m of single thread and attach to the flower motif bringing the needle through to emerge from the A bead at the tip of the lowest petal (fig 13).

13 Thread on 1F, 10A, 1B, 1C, 1B, 1A, 1E, 1A, 1B, 1C, 1B, 1A, 1E, 1A, 1B, 1C, 1B, 1A, 1E, 1A, 1B, 1C, 1B, 1A, 1E, 1A, 1D, 1B, 2D, 1C, 1J, 1C, 1D, 1A, 1B, 1A, 1D, 1K, 1D, 1A, 1C, 1A, 2D, 1H and 4D.

fig 14   fig 15

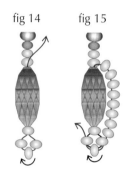

14 Leaving aside the last 3D beads threaded to form an anchor pass the needle through the first 1D of the 4D beads and the following H bead to form a picot at the bottom of the strand (fig 14).

Thread on 8D. Pass the needle through the 3D beads of the picot (fig 15).

15 Thread on 8D. Pass the needle down through the H bead, the following 1D and the 3D of the picot. Pass the needle back up through the 1D bead and the H bead (fig 16) to complete a leaf frame around the H bead.

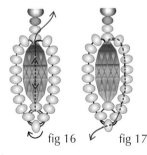

fig 16   fig 17

16 Pass the needle through the 8D beads added in step 14 and the first 2D of the picot (fig 17).

Thread on 1B, 2D, 1H and 4D. Make a 3D picot at the bottom as before bringing the needle back through the 1D and 1H beads (fig 18).

Complete a leaf frame around this H bead as in figs 15 and 16.

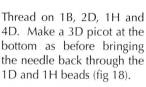

fig 18   fig 19

Following fig 19 pass the needle up through the 2D and 1B beads above this leaf and the beads of the picot and leaf motif above to emerge from the top of the first H bead (fig 19).

17 Pass the needle back up through all of the strand beads above the leaf motif to emerge from the F bead at the top. Pass the needle through the A bead at the tip of the flower petal picot in the same direction as before to centralise the strand below this bead (see fig 20).

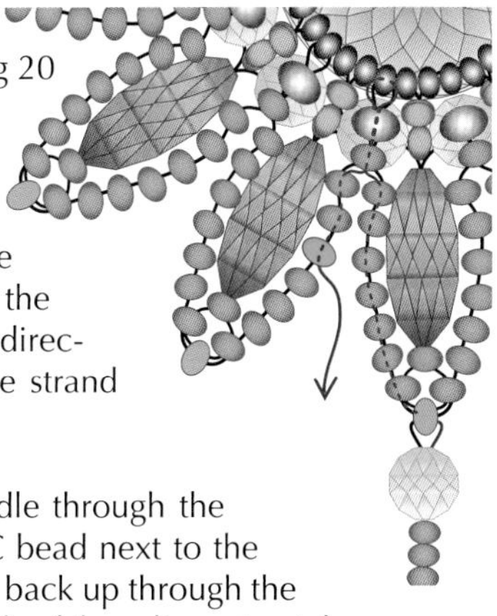

fig 20

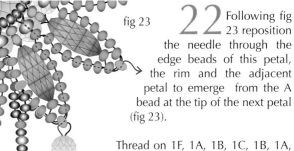

Following fig 20 pass the needle through the edge beads of this petal, the C bead next to the rim, the B bead on the rim and back up through the C bead and the near edge beads of the adjacent petal to emerge from the fourth A bead (fig 20).

18 Thread on 3B, 1A, 1B, 1C, 1B, 1A, 1E, 1A, 1B, 1C, 1B, 1A, 1E, 1A, 1B, 1C, 1B, 1A, 1E, 1A, 1D, 1B, 1D, 1K, 1D, 1A, 1C, 1A, 2D, 1H and 4D.
Repeat steps 14, 15 and 16.

19 Pass the needle back up through the strand beads above the leaf motif to emerge between the top A bead of the strand and the top 3B beads (fig 21).

Fig 21 shows the A beads of the underside petal edge. You can see the second of the two corresponding A beads designated to support the strand on the petal edges marked in a darker blue.

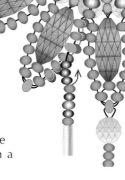

fig 21

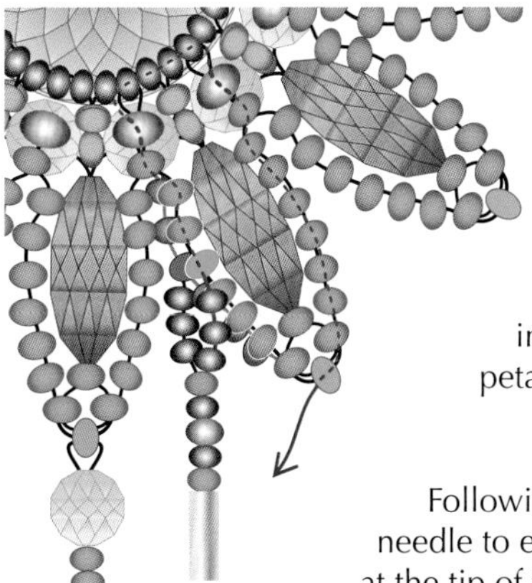

20 Flip the flower over and referring to fig 22 thread on 3B and pass the needle through the indicated A bead on this petal edge to centralise the strand below.

Following fig 22 reposition the needle to emerge from the A bead at the tip of the same petal ready to make the next fringe strand.

fig 22

21 Thread on 1F, 5A, 1B, 1C, 1B, 1A, 1E, 1A, 1B, 1C, 1B, 1A, 1E, 1A, 1B, 1C, 1B, 1A, 1E, 1A, 1B, 1C, 1B, 1A, 1E, 1A, 1D, 1B, 2D, 1C, 1J, 1C, 1D, 1A, 1B, 1A, 1D, 1K, 1D, 1A, 1C, 1A, 2D, 1H and 4D.

Repeat steps 14, 15 and 16.

Pass the needle up through the remaining beads of the strand and through the A bead at the tip of the picot in the same direction as before to centralise the strand beneath this bead.

fig 23

22 Following fig 23 reposition the needle through the edge beads of this petal, the rim and the adjacent petal to emerge from the A bead at the tip of the next petal (fig 23).

Thread on 1F, 1A, 1B, 1C, 1B, 1A, 1E, 1A, 1D, 1B, 1D, 1K, 1D, 1A, 1C, 1A, 2D, 1H and 4D.

Repeat steps 14, 15 and 16.

Complete the strand as before passing the needle through the A bead at the tip of the petal to centralise the strand properly.

Finish off the thread ends neatly and securely.

Use a new thread to make three matching strands (as steps 17 - 22) on the other side of the long central strand.

23
The Hanging Loop - Prepare the needle with 2m of single thread and attach to the flower bringing the needle through to emerge from the A bead at the tip of the top petal (fig 24).

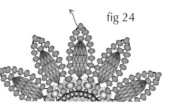

fig 24

Thread on 1B, 1C, 1A, 1L, 1A, 1C, 1B, 25D, 1H and 4D.

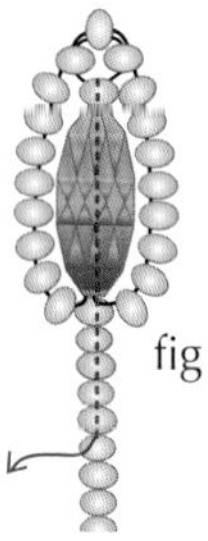

24
Following steps 14 and 15 create a leaf motif around this H bead. Pass the needle through the first 5D beads below the H bead (fig 25). This fifth D bead will support two more leaf motifs.

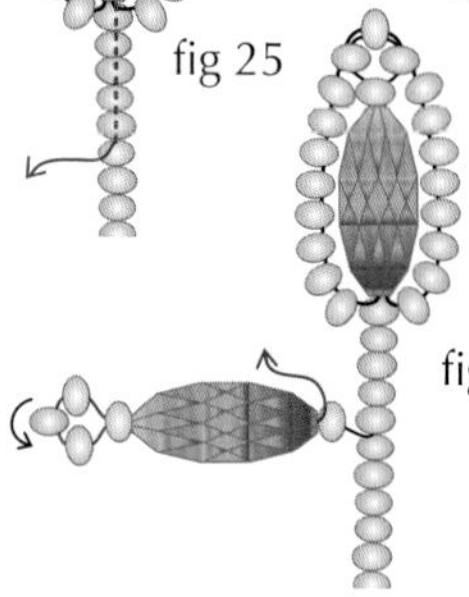

fig 25

25
Thread on 1D, 1H and 4D. As before leave aside the last 3D to form the anchor and pass back through the previous 1D and 1H (fig 26).

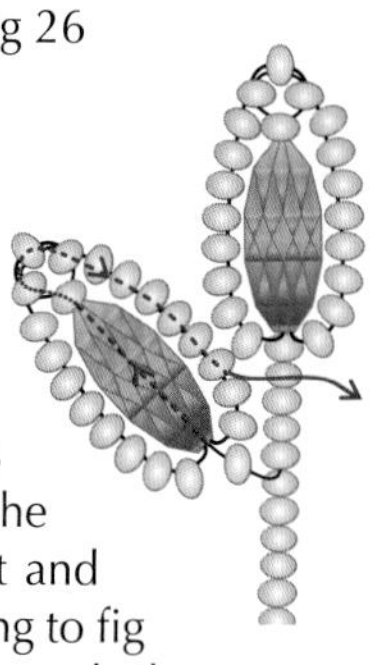

fig 26

fig 27

26
Thread on 8D. Pass the needle through the 3D beads of the picot and thread on 8D. Referring to fig 27 pass the needle through the H bead, the following 1D, the 3D of the picot and the first six D beads down the side of the motif (fig 27).

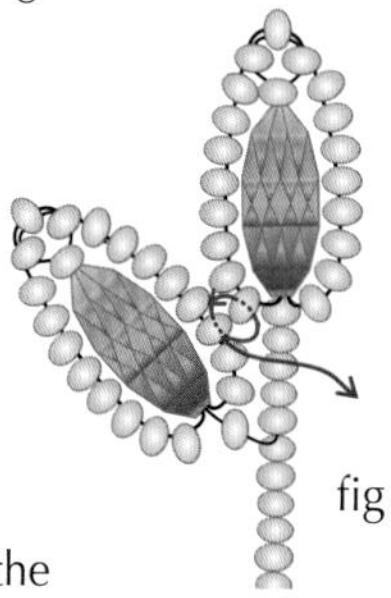

This sixth D bead needs to be linked to the first leaf motif with a square stitch.

Referring to fig 28 pass the needle through the first D bead on the closest edge of the adjacent motif and back through the sixth D bead on this motif making a square stitch (fig 28).

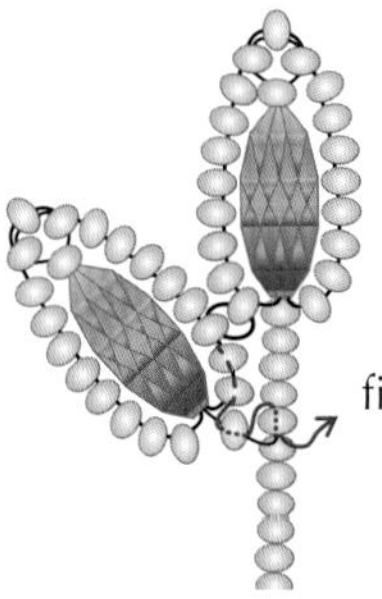

fig 28

Pass the needle around this stitch path again to make the link stronger.

Pass the needle through the last 2D along the side of the motif, the 1D at the base of the H bead and the 1D on the main strand in the same direction as before (fig 29).

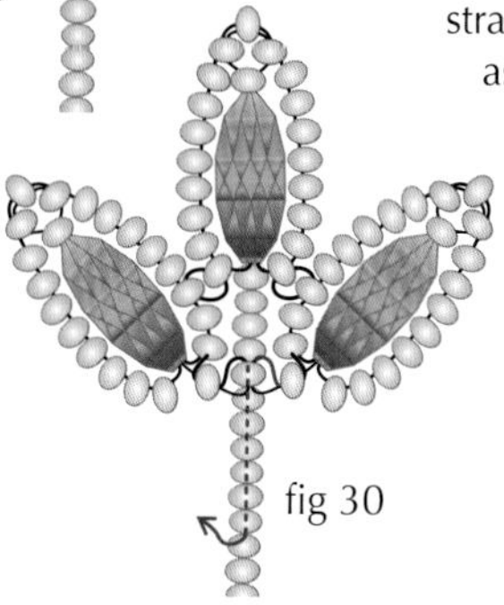

fig 29

27
Repeat steps 25 and 26 to make a new leaf motif supported on this D bead to the other side of the main strand (see fig 30).

fig 30

Pass the needle through the following 6D of the main stem (fig 30). This sixth D bead will support another pair of leaf motifs.

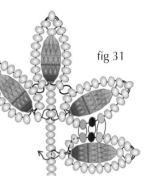

28
Repeat step 25 to start a new motif.

fig 31

Refer to fig 31, where you can see the new motif and the three links you need to make to the adjacent leaf - the three pairs of D beads are marked in contrasting colours to make the connections more visible.

Make the first strap of 8D as before passing through the 3D beads of the picot. With reference to fig 27 thread on the second 8D and pass through the H bead, around the picot and through the first 4D beads of the first 8D strap to emerge through the bead marked yellow in fig 31. Square stitch this bead to the bead marked yellow on the adjacent leaf motif.

Pass the needle through the next D bead along the new leaf motif (marked blue) and square stitch that bead to the corresponding blue bead on the adjacent motif.

Repeat for the paired D beads marked brown on fig 31.

Pass the needle through to emerge from the D bead on the main strand (fig 31).

Repeat step 28 to make a matching leaf motif to the other side of the main strand making the appropriate links to the adjacent motif. Finish with the needle emerging from the D bead on the main stem as fig 31.

29
Pass the needle through the following 6D of the main strand. Repeat step 28 to make another pair of leaf motifs linked to the previous motifs as in fig 31.*

Pass the needle through the following 4D of the main strand - this D bead will support two smaller leaf shapes.

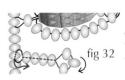

30 Thread on 7D. Leaving aside the last 3D beads threaded to form a picot pass the needle back through the first 4D beads and the D bead on the main strand (fig 32).

fig 32

31 Pass the needle through the first 1D of the 7D added in step 30 and thread on 4D. Pass the needle through the 3D beads of the picot (fig 33).

fig 33

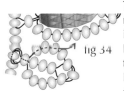

Thread on 4D. Following fig 34 pass the needle through the first 1D bead added in step 30 to emerge at the main strand. Pass the needle through the D bead on the main strand, back through the first D of this motif and the first 3D of the first side strap (fig 34).

fig 34

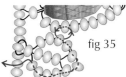

This third D bead needs to be linked with a square stitch to the third D bead of the adjacent leaf motif. Following fig 35 make the link. Make the link stronger with a second pass of the needle.

fig 35

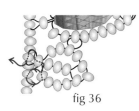

Pass the needle through the beads around the edge of the small motif to emerge as shown on fig 35. This last D bead needs to link to the second D bead down the main strap with a square stitch. Make the stitch as shown in fig 36 bringing the needle through to emerge from the D bead on the main strand.

fig 36

Repeat steps 30 and 31 to make a second matching small leaf motif on the other side of the main strand.

Pass the needle down through the remaining 2D and the following beads of the main strand to emerge at the top of the flower.

32 Pass the needle through the A bead at the tip of the petal picot and back up the beads of the hanging loop strand to emerge from the top B bead (fig 37). You now need to make a matching nine leaf frond as made in steps 24 to 31. These two fronds are linked together at the top with 1C bead.

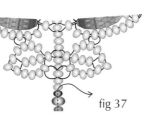

fig 37

33 Thread on 25D, 1H, 3D and 1C. Pass the needle through the 1D at the tip of the top leaf motif made in step 25 (fig 38).

Following fig 39 pass the needle through the C bead in the same direction as before and the last D bead added. Thread on 1D and pass through the D bead adjacent to the H bead to complete a picot (fig 39).

fig 38

fig 39

The tips of the two strands are now linked together through the C bead.

34 Pass the needle through the H bead. You are now in the correct position to start the first of the leaf motifs to the side of the main strand.

Repeat from step 24 to step 31 inclusive.

To finish off the hanging loop you need to strengthen the stitches to the A bead at the tip of the petal and the C bead link between the tips of the leaf fronds. Pass the needle through the A bead at the tip of the flower motif and up through the beads of the first main strand to emerge at the C bead. Pass through the figure-of-eight linkage as shown in figs 38 and 39 at least three times. Pass down the other main strand and through the A bead at the tip of the flower petal again.

Finish off the thread end and all other remaining loose ends neatly and securely.

Heligan Inspirations
Babylon Necklace

An opulent necklace design using the Heligan flower in two sizes, Heligan leaf fronds, fringe strands and an exotic colour palette.

The materials list is quite long but you can rationalise by using just one colour each of the 4mm faceted glass & size 8/o seed beads throughout

You Will Need

Materials

8g of size 10/0 silver lined magenta seed beads A
7g of size 10/0 transparent garnet AB seed beads B
3g of size 8/0 transparent turquoise AB seed beads C
12g of size 10/0 silver lined capri blue seed beads D
1g of size 3 silver lined capri blue bugle beads E
Twelve 4mm capri blue AB fire polished faceted beads F
Twelve 8x6mm red AB crystal oval beads G
Eighteen 8x6mm purple scarab crystal oval beads H
6g of size 10/0 silver lined orange seed beads J
3g of size 8/0 silver lined magenta seed beads K
3g of size 8/0 frost silver lined cerise AB seed beads L
One 18mm Colorado topaz AB cushioned oval disc M
Two 14mm Black Russian AB cushion crystal discs N
Ten 4mm pink fire polished faceted beads P
Ten 4mm garnet AB fire polished faceted beads Q
Twenty 6x4mm turquoise AB oval crystal beads R
Four 6x4mm blue scarab crystal rondelle beads S
One 6x4mm red crystal rondelle bead T
One 8x6mm red crystal rondelle bead U
One 8x6mm turquoise crystal rondelle bead V
Two 8mm red crystal beads W
One 8mm blue scarab crystal bead X
A reel of navy blue size D beading thread
A reel of red size D beading thread

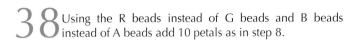

The Necklace is Made in Six Stages -
The large central flower motif.
The two smaller flower motifs.
The leaf motifs.
The assembly of the central part of the design.
The tassel stranding.
The side straps and the clasp.

35 The Large Central Flower - Follow steps 1 to 11 inclusive to make the central flower of the design using the red thread. Finish the thread ends neatly and securely and set this motif aside for the moment.

36 The Smaller Flower Motifs - The basic method for the smaller flowers is the same as for the central flower but there is an alteration in the bead counts.

Refer to steps 1 to 11 throughout.

For the first small flower prepare the needle with red thread as in step 1 and thread on 1N, 1B, 1P, 1B, 1P, 1B, 1P, 1B, 1P and 1B. Pass the needle through the N bead to make a strap to the side.

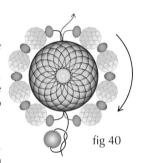

fig 40

Thread on 1B, 1P, 1B, 1P, 1B, 1P, 1B, 1P and 1B. Pass the needle through the N bead to make a strap to the other side of the N bead (fig 40).

As in step 3 add 1P bead into the gaps above the hole in the larger N bead (fig 41).

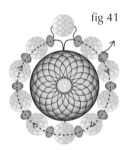

fig 41

Note that the number of 4mm beads has dropped from twelve on the large flower to ten on this smaller size.

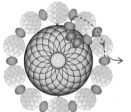

fig 42

37 The inner rim bead count also needs to be altered.

Thread on 1B, 2J and 1B. Make the stitch as in step 4 (fig 42).

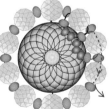

fig 43

Thread on 1B and 3J. Make the stitch as before passing the needle through the first 1B of the previous stitch and the following 1P, 1B and 1P (fig 43).

Make the next stitch with 1B and 2J.

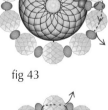

fig 44

Alternate the last two stitches around the circle closing up the sequence with a 3J stitch (fig 44). You will have added 25J in total.

Pass the needle through the J beads to bring them into a neat circle.

Repeat on the other side of the N bead as before.

38 Using the R beads instead of G beads and B beads instead of A beads add 10 petals as in step 8.

Reposition the needle to emerge from the second J bead of the first stitch made in step 37.

39 As the J bead count on the inner rim between the B beads alternates between 2J and 3J, the connection to the base of the petal frames will need to change slightly.

Thread on 1K and 5B. Pass the needle through the 3B beads of the picot at the tip of the R bead. Thread on 5B and 1K. Pass the needle through the middle J bead of the next 3J beads around the rim (see fig 45).

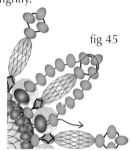

fig 45

Pass the needle back up though the last 1K and 1B beads added (fig 45).

Thread on 4B and pass through the 3B picot at the tip of the next R bead and thread on 5B and 1K.

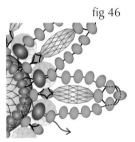

fig 46

Pass the needle through the 2J beads on the rim and back up through the last 1K and 1B beads (fig 46). This centres the K bead above the 2J beads on the rim.

Work around the flower with this slight adjustment on the alternate petals and link the last petal frame to the first petal frame as before. Pass the needle through the J beads of the rim to neaten the circle.

As on the large petal, pass the needle through to the other side of the N bead and repeat the petal frames around the R beads on this side. Finish off the thread ends neatly and securely.

40 Repeat to make a second flower using the N and R beads as before but substituting -

the B beads for J beads
the J beads for A beads
the L beads for K beads
the Q beads for P beads.

41 The Leaf Motifs - Prepare the needle with 1.5m of single blue thread and tie a keeper bead 15cm from the end. Thread on 25D, 1H and 4D.

Follow steps 24 to the * in step 29 to make a seven leaf frond. Pass the needle through the remaining beads of the main strand to emerge alongside the keeper bead. Remove the needle and put this frond aside for the moment.

42 Prepare the needle as in step 41 and thread on 20D, 1H and 4D.

Make the first five leaves as step 41. Make the sixth leaf in the same position as in step 41 but do not link to the adjacent leaf.

Pass the needle through the remaining beads of the main stem to complete a six leaf frond (fig 47). Remove the needle.

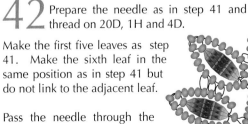
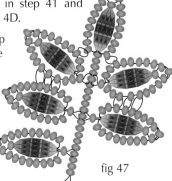

fig 47

43 Assembling the Central Design - The three flower motifs and the two leaf motifs are stitched together through the tips of the petals, the tips of the leaves and the ends of the frond stems. You will need to use a single thread but to make each stitch firm the needle will have to pass through the beads several times. Use both colours of thread - the exact position of your stitches will determine which colour is most appropriate.

Fig 48 shows the back of the assembly plan. Lay out your flowers and leaf fronds as shown. The five items need to be stitched together but the threads neither tied nor trimmed until the whole arrangement is linked and you are happy with the siting of all of the elements.

fig 48

44 Use the tail threads on the leaf fronds to stitch the ends of the fronds onto the inner rims of both the large and small flower.

Use a red thread to stitch the right-hand flower to the two leaf tips as shown. Push the petal sitting between the leaf tips further into the gap and secure to the sides of the two leaves with a few stitches.

45 Use a red thread to link the left-hand and central flowers together pushing the larger petal between the two smaller petals so you can make a very firm join.

The long frond to the right will need to be secured to the outside edges of the large flower - make a few stitches in blue thread to catch the petal edges onto the leaves and stem.

The loose leaf on the left hand frond will now need to be secured to the adjacent leaf - it was left detached in step 41 to give flexibility to the frond stem. Bring it up against the adjacent leaf and stitch into place with blue thread.

46 Turn the work over and check the arrangement. You may wish to alter some of the connections - a bead to the left or the right can make a big difference to how it all sits together. When you are happy with the placings secure all of the thread ends, neaten and trim without blocking the holes on the inner rim of the large flower.

47 The Tassel - Prepare the needle with 1.5m of single blue thread and attach to the inner rim on the back of the large flower. Pass the needle through these B beads to emerge 2B below the attachment position of the leaf frond.

Sort through the D beads to find one bead with a slightly larger hole than average - thread this bead onto the needle. This will be the tassel top or head bead.

48 Thread on 25D, 1J, 1A, 1C, 1A, 1J, 1E, 1B, 1C, 1B, 1S, 1B, 2D, 1H and 4D.

Follow steps 14 to 16 to convert this H bead into a leaf motif and to add a second leaf motif swapping the B bead for a K bead on the link between the two leaves for an extra splash of colour.

Pass the needle back up through the beads of the strand to emerge just before the larger-holed D bead added in step 47.

Pass up through the tassel top D bead and the B bead on the rim.

Pass back down the tassel top D bead ready to start the next strand (fig 49).

fig 49

49 For the next strand thread on 15D, 1J, 1A, 1C, 1A, 1J, 1E, 1B, 1S, 1B, 2D, 1H and 4D. Follow figs 14, 15 and 16 to make a single leaf motif and pass the needle back up to the top of the strand. Pass through the tassel top D bead, through the B bead on the rim and back down the tassel top bead ready to make the next strand.

50 Thread on 8D, 1J, 1A, 1C, 1A, 1J, 1E, 1B, 1C, 1B, 1S, 1B, 2D, 1H and 4D. Complete the strand as in step 49.

Thread on 2D, 1J, 1A, 1C, 1A, 1J, 1E, 1B, 1C, 1B, 1S, 1B, 2D, 1H and 4D. Complete the strand as in step 49.

Finish off the thread end neatly and securely.

51 The Side Straps & the Clasp - Prepare the needle with 1.5m of single blue thread and tie a keeper bead 15cm from the end.

Thread on 1W and 7A. Pass the needle through the W bead to pull the A beads into a strap around the side of the W bead (fig 50).

fig 50

Thread on 7B and pass the needle through the W bead to make a B bead strap alongside the A bead strap. Repeat to make a third strap from 7J.

Repeat these three straps two more times to completely cover the W bead with an alternating stripe pattern.

52 Thread on 1C, 1U, 1K and 1B. Pass the needle through the D bead at the tip of the end leaf motif as shown on the left in fig 48. Thread on 1B. Pass the needle back through the K bead (fig 51).

Pass the needle through the following 1U, 1C, the covered W bead and thread on 1C and 1A.

fig 51

Mix the remaining D beads with a tiny sprinkle of A and J beads - this mix is used for the main part of the strap - call it Z.

Thread on sufficient of these Z beads to reach the centre back of your preferred necklace length.

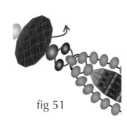

53 Thread on 1C, 1T, 1C and 19B. Pass the needle back through the 1C, 1T and 1C beads to draw the B beads into a loop (fig 52).

fig 52

Thread on the same number of Z beads as before to bring the needle back to the other end of the strap. Pass the needle through the 1A, 1C, the covered W bead and the following 1C, 1U, 1K and 1B. Pass the needle through the D bead at the tip of the leaf and back up through the 1B, 1K, 1U, 1C, the covered W bead, 1C and 1A beads ready to add another Z bead strap.

54 Thread on the same number of Z beads again and pass the needle through the 1C, 1T and 1C beads before the loop, through the 19B of the loop and back through the 1C, 1T and 1C beads. Add a fourth strap of Z beads.

Continue to add a fifth and a sixth strap in a similar manner.

Finish off the thread ends neatly and securely.

55 Repeat steps 51 and 52 substituting a V bead for the U bead. Attach this strap to the small flower on the right in fig 48 passing the needle through the third petal tip along the top edge. When you reach the centre back you will need to add a bead tag.

Thread on 1K, 1J, 1X, 1J, 1C, 1A, 1B and 1A.

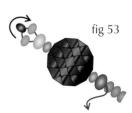

fig 53

Pass the needle back down the C bead and the following 1J, 1X, 1J and 1K to emerge at the end of the Z bead strap (fig 53).

Work backwards and forwards as for the previous side strap to complete six Z bead straps in total.

Finish off all remaining thread ends neatly and securely.

Balmoral Tassel

You Will Need

Materials

10g of size 10/0 silver lined capri blue seed beads A
8g of size 10/0 lustre mustard seed beads B
8g of size 6/0 metallic bronze AB seed beads C
5g of size 3 silver lined brown bugle beads D
Twenty-nine 6x4mm blue scarab crystal rondelles E
Fourteen 8x6mm blue scarab crystal rondelles F
One 18mm round wooden base bead
50cm of stranded beading wire
Two gilt French crimps
A reel of black size D beading thread
A piece of paper approximately 40x100mm in size

Tools

A size 10 beading needle
A pair of scissors to trim the threads
A pair of flat-faced pliers or crimping pliers

*The finished length of this tassel is 26cm
including the hanging loop.
It measures 16cm below the hanging loop.*

The golden brown bracken and deep inky blue lochs of a Scottish Highland Autumn are brought together in the palette for this beaded bead tassel. If you have not made a fancy beaded bead before this is a good one to start with - it takes a little time but the technique is straightforward and the result is very versatile.

The Tassel is Made in Four Stages

The large base bead is covered with a beaded net.
The tassel stranding below the large bead is created.
The small beaded bead decoration to go above the large bead is made.
The whole decoration is then brought together with the addition of the hanging loop.

1 The Large Beaded Bead - Examine the large wooden bead - you may be able to see small wooden fibres pushing into the hole and around the edges of the hole - it is important that the hole is smooth. Push a knitting needle, or similar, through the hole to smooth the fibres.

To prevent the seed beads from going down the hole of the base bead roll the 40x100mm piece of paper and line the hole in the wooden bead. Prepare the needle with 2m of single thread and anchor the end 15cm to the paper tube with a double stitch. Pass the needle through the wooden bead ready to start the netting. This bead will now be referred to as the large base bead.

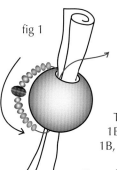

fig 1

2 Thread on 4A, 1B, 1C, 1B, 1E, 1B, 1C, 1B and 4A.

Pass the needle through the large base bead to make a strap around the side (fig 1).

Thread on 1A, 1B, 1C, 1B, 1E, 1B, 1C, 1B, 1E, 1B, 1C, 1B and 1A.

Pass the needle through the large base bead to make a second strap alongside the first one (fig 2).

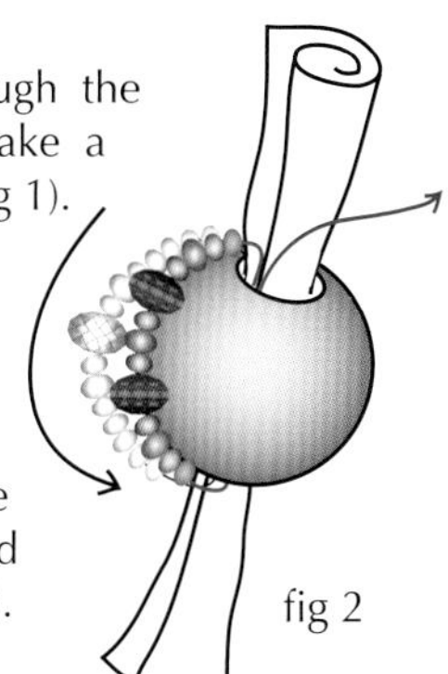

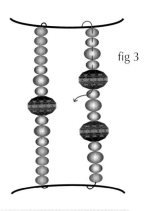

fig 2

For simplicity figs 2 to 14 will show the straps lying parallel to one another - on your work the straps will come closer together at the top and at the bottom.

3 Pass the needle through the first five beads of the strap just made to emerge from the first crystal E bead of the second strap (fig 3).

To create the netted effect the E beads from this strap will be linked across to the C beads on the previous strap and vice versa.

fig 3

Extra Info....

If you are working with pale seed beads or transparent crystals you may wish to paint the wooden base bead with a matching pale tone before you start to work. This will show through the beads and enhance the colour throughout the whole design.

4 Thread on 3B and 1A. Pass the needle though the top C bead of the previous strap (fig 4).

fig 4

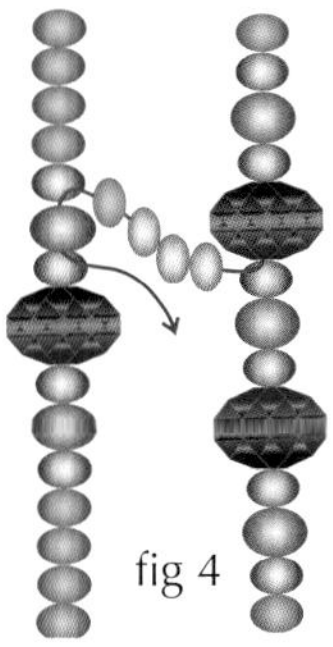

Thread on 1A. Pass the needle through the last B bead of the beads just added in the opposite direction (fig 5).

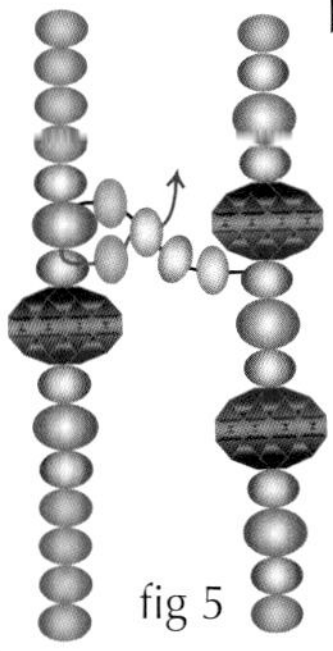

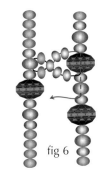

fig 5

5 Thread on 2B. Pass the needle through the E bead on the last strap made in the same direction as before and the following 1B and 1C to emerge from the next C bead on this strap (fig 6).

fig 6

6 Thread on 1A and 4B. Pass the needle through the middle E bead on the previous strap (fig 7).

fig 7

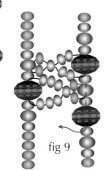

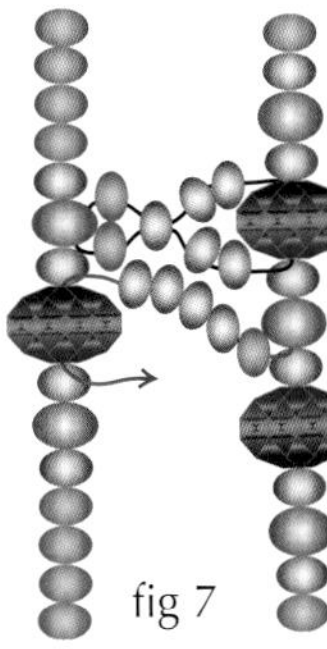

Thread on 3B. Pass the needle through the first B bead of the beads just added in the opposite direction (fig 8).

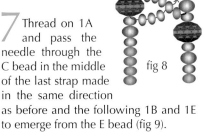

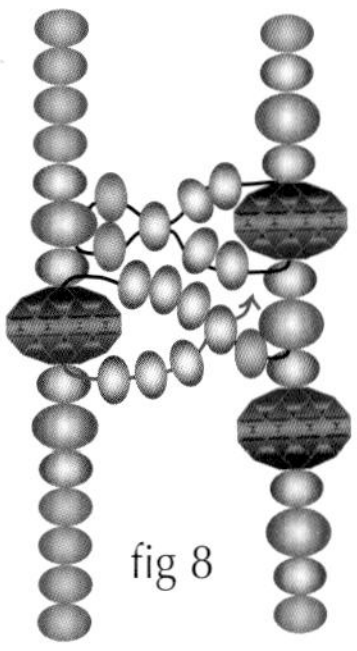

fig 8

7 Thread on 1A and pass the needle through the C bead in the middle of the last strap made in the same direction as before and the following 1B and 1E to emerge from the E bead (fig 9).

fig 9

Note that on the first connection the sequence was 1B bead shorter on each arm - this shapes the beadwork to give a snug fit over the large base bead.

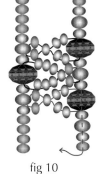

fig 10

8 The last connection between these two straps is between the E bead the needle is emerging from and the remaining C bead on the previous strap.

Make this connection following the same sequence as step 4 and step 5 bringing the needle through to emerge from the bottom of the last strap made on completion (fig 10).

Pass the needle through the large base bead.

9 Thread on 4A, 1B, 1C, 1B, 1E, 1B, 1C, 1B and 4A. Pass the needle through the large base bead to draw this new strap alongside the previous strap.

This new strap now needs to be connected to the previous strap. Pass the needle through the first six beads of the strap to emerge through the first C bead (see fig 11)

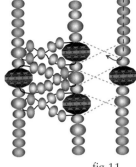

fig 11

Fig 11 shows the paths of the connections to be made between this new strap and the previous strap.

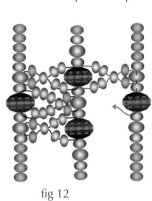

fig 12

10 Make the first connection by threading on 1A and 3B. Pass the needle through the first E bead on the previous strap.

Thread on 2B. Pass the needle through the first B bead of the 3B just added and thread on 1A.

Pass the needle through the C bead on the new strap and the following 1A and 1E (fig 12).

You can see this is a mirror image of the connection made in figs 4-6. The E bead on the second strap is now framed by the B beads.

11 For the second connection thread on 4B and 1A. Pass the needle through the C bead at the centre of the previous strap.

Thread on 1A and pass the needle through the last B bead of the 4B beads just added. Thread on 3B.

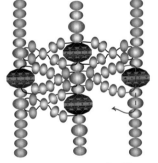

fig 13

Pass the needle through the E bead at the centre of the new strap and the following 1B and 1C (fig 13).

You can see this is a mirror image of the connection made in figs 7-9.

12 For the third connection thread on 1A and 3B. Pass the needle through the last E bead on the previous strap.

Thread on 2B. Pass the needle through the first B bead of the 3B beads just added and thread on 1A.

Pass the needle through the last C bead of the new strap and the following 1B and 4A (fig 14). Pass the needle through the large base bead.

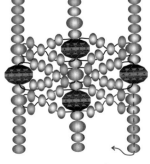

fig 14

You can see this is a mirror image of the connection made in fig 10. The E bead on the previous strap is now framed by the B beads.

13 Thread on 1A, 1B, 1C, 1B, 1E, 1B, 1C, 1B, 1E, 1B, 1C, 1B and 1A. Pass through the large base bead to make the next strap alongside the previous strap.

14 Repeat from step 3 to step 13 inclusive twice. Repeat from the beginning of step 3 to step 8 inclusive.

You will now have four repeats of each strap pattern. The last strap worked (with 2E beads) needs to be connected to the first strap worked in step 2 (a 1E bead strap).

Pass the needle down through the first six beads of the first strap to emerge from the first C of the strap (as fig 11). Make the connections to the last strap worked as in step 10 to step 12 inclusive.

If you examine the work so far you will see that the equator of the large bead is covered very well but there are gaps between the straps near to the hole on both ends of the beaded bead - you will need to make a series of small stitches to finish off the netting here.

15 Make sure that the needle has emerged between the end of two straps at the edge of the hole on the large base bead. Examine the adjacent strap which contains two E beads - the top E bead of this strap will have a diamond-shaped frame of B beads surrounding it. Locate the two beads on this frame immediately to either side of the top B bead on the strap - these are the beads that will support the small stitches you are about to make.

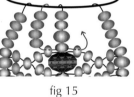

fig 15

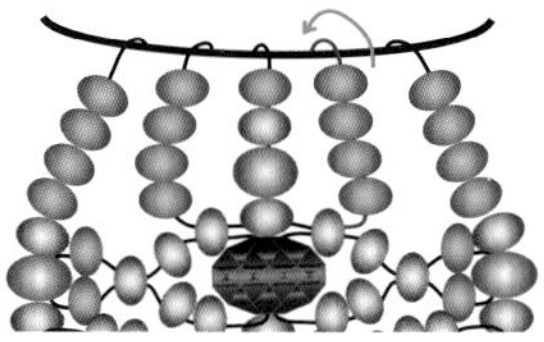

fig 16

16 Thread on 4A. Following fig 15 pass the needle through the first of these B beads on the diamond; pass the needle under the strap just above the E bead and through the following 1B on the other side of the diamond (fig 15). Thread on 4A and pass the needle through the large base bead to draw the new 4A into the required gap as shown in fig 16.

17 Repeat steps 15 and 16 at the other end of the same strap.

Repeat steps 16 and 17 three more times to add these extra short rows to each of the straps containing 2E beads.

Undo the anchor stitches made through the paper tube. Tie off the thread ends but do not trim the tails yet - leave them until the whole tassel has been completed just in case you catch a thread and snag the design during the final assembly. Set the beaded bead aside. DO NOT REMOVE THE PAPER TUBE as the small beads can still fall inside the large hole: wait until you are ready for the final tassel assembly when the tube will be replaced, with an F bead at either end, which will stabilise the design properly.

18 The Tassel Strands - On the finished design the tassel strands are held together just below the beaded bead by an F bead. The stranding is made as a separate unit with the F bead at the top - the F bead is then pulled into place during final assembly.

Prepare the needle with 2m of single thread.

Tip out your C beads and choose one bead with a larger than average hole.

Tip out your F beads and choose two beads with the largest hole size. Put one aside for the small beaded bead (see below) - you will use the other F bead for the top of this tassel.

Tie the selected C bead to the thread 15cm from the end with a secure double knot and thread on the tassel top F bead - these two beads form the top of the stranding.

For the tassel strand thread on - 14A, 3B, 3A, 2B, 5A, 1B, 1D, 1A, 1D, 1A, 1B, 1A, 1D, 1A, 1B, 1A, 1C, 1A, 1C, 1A, 1B, 1E, 1B, 1A, 1C, 1F, 1A, 1C, 1A, 1B and 13A. Leaving aside the last 13A threaded to form a loop pass the needle back up though the last B bead threaded and all of the following beads to emerge at the top of the strand - pass the needle through the F bead (fig 17).

Adjust the tension in the thread so that the strand falls softly but no thread is showing beneath the F bead or between the F bead and the C bead at the very top.

Pass the needle through the C bead above the F bead and back down the F bead ready to start the next strand (fig 18).

fig 17

fig 18

19 Repeat step 18 until you have made eleven tassel strands in total - finish with the needle emerging from the top of the F bead adjacent to the C bead.

Tie the needle end of the thread to the tail thread left at the beginning of step 18 with a secure double knot. Pass the needle down through the F bead and, if you wish, through a few beads at the top of one of the tassel strands before trimming close to neaten. Repeat with the other tail(s) of thread.

Set the stranding aside.

20 The Small Beaded Bead - Prepare the needle with 1m of single thread and tie a keeper bead 15cm from the end.

Thread on the larger-holed F bead that you have saved for this beaded bead - this will be the base bead for this beaded bead.

Thread on 2A, 1B, 1E, 1B and 2A. Pass the needle through the F bead to form a strap around the outside of the F bead (fig 19).

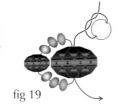

fig 19

21 Thread on 2B, 1A, 1C, 1A and 2B. Pass the needle through the F bead to make a second strap (fig 20). Push this strap to sit alongside the first strap.

fig 20

This pair of strap sequences form the pattern for this beaded bead. Repeat the pattern three more times to give you four repeats of the two straps right around the F bead.

Pass the needle through one of the beaded straps so that it emerges alongside the keeper bead. Remove the keeper and tie the two thread ends together securely. Do not neaten and trim yet - leave until the complete tassel is assembled.

22 The Hanging Loop - Unravel the stranded beading wire and examine the cut ends - it is important that the ends are cut cleanly so they cannot snag on the threads inside the beaded beads - if necessary trim them neatly.

Pass the wire through the C bead at the top of the tassel stranding made in steps 18 and 19 positioning it at the centre of the length.

Carefully remove the paper tube from the large beaded bead. Pass the wire ends through the beaded bead - if you do this one end at a time you are less likely to snag the fine beading threads inside the beaded bead.

Pass both ends of the wire through 1F.

Pull up both ends of the wire and push down the last F bead threaded so that the C bead at the top of the tassel pulls up inside the large beaded bead and the two F beads nestle snugly against the holes at either end of the beaded bead (fig 21).

fig 21

23 Pass both ends of the wire through 1C, 1B and 1E. One at a time, pass the ends through the small beaded bead made in steps 20 and 21. Thread on 1E and make sure that the E beads at either end of the small beaded bead sit snugly against the hole. Thread on 1B and 1C.

Separate the wire ends to make the loop.

Onto the first end thread 4A, 1B, 1C, 1B, 5A, 1B, 1C, 1B, 7A, 1B, 1C, 1B, 9A, 1B, 1C, 1B, 11A, 1B, 1C, 1B, 13A, 1B, 1C, 1B, and 15A.

Onto the other end thread 7A, 1B, 1C, 1B, 7A, 1B, 1C, 1B, 9A, 1B, 1C, 1B, 11A, 1B, 1C, 1B, 13A, 1B, 1C, 1B, and 15A. This will give you a staggered pattern of 1B, 1C , 1B blocks up both sides of the hanging loop. If you require a longer (or shorter) loop make any neccessary adjustment to the bead count now.

fig 22

Thread one French crimp, 1C and a second French crimp onto one end of the wire. Pass the other end of the wire in the opposite direction through these three components (fig 22). Pull on the two ends of the wire to take up any slack in the hanging loop and the sequence between the beaded beads.
Squash both crimps flat to grip the wire and make everything secure.

If possible pass the ends of the wire through a few A beads to either side to neaten before trimming (this is a tight fit so you may not manage it). Trim the wire ends as close as possible to the work.

24 Return to the thread ends left on the beaded beads. Re-attach the needle to each end in turn and pass through a few beads of an adjacent strap around the beaded bead before trimming neatly.

Heather Earrings

Make earrings to match the Heather Necklace.

Make two small beaded beads following steps 20 and 21.

Use a headpin for the bottom link threading on a size 10/0 and a 6/0 bead first. Then add a small beaded bead, an 8x6mm crystal rondelle and a size 10/0 seed bead. Trim the pin to 8mm above the top bead and make a loop.

Link this loop to an eyepin and thread on one 6x4mm crystal rondelle sandwiched between two size 10/0 seed beads. Trim to 8mm above the top bead, make the loop and add the earfitting.

Galloway Pin

Make a larger beaded bead as in fig 23. Thread a 6x4mm crystal rondelle onto an 80mm stick pin. Thread on the larger beaded bead, another 6x4mm crystal rondelle and a size 10/0 seed bead. Use a French crimp to secure the beads in place at the top of the pin.

Moray Tassel

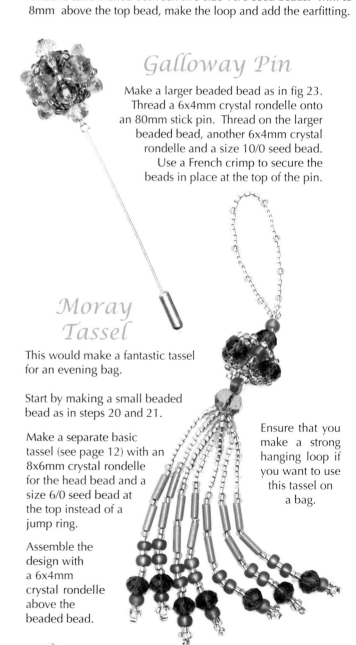

This would make a fantastic tassel for an evening bag.

Start by making a small beaded bead as in steps 20 and 21.

Make a separate basic tassel (see page 12) with an 8x6mm crystal rondelle for the head bead and a size 6/0 seed bead at the top instead of a jump ring.

Assemble the design with a 6x4mm crystal rondelle above the beaded bead.

Ensure that you make a strong hanging loop if you want to use this tassel on a bag.

You Will Need

Materials

5ml of size 10/0 silver lined lime seed beads A
5ml of size 10/0 silver lined eau de nil seed beads B
5ml of size 10/0 silver lined pale teal seed beads C
5ml of size 10/0 transparent turquoise AB seed beads D
Fourteen 8x6mm milky eau de nil crystal rondelles E
Four 8x6mm turquoise crystal rondelles F
Eleven 8x6mm pale tanzanite crystal rondelles G
Ten 8x6mm teal crystal rondelles H
Thirty-four 6x4mm eau de nil crystal rondelles J
Twenty-six 6x4mm turquoise crystal rondelles K
Thirty-four 6x4mm dark tanzanite crystal rondelles L
Two 6x4mm teal crystal rondelles M
3ml of size 6/0 transparent lime AB seed beads N
3ml of size 6/0 transparent turquoise seed beads P
60cm of stranded beading wire
Two silver-plated French crimps
A reel of sterling grey size D beading thread

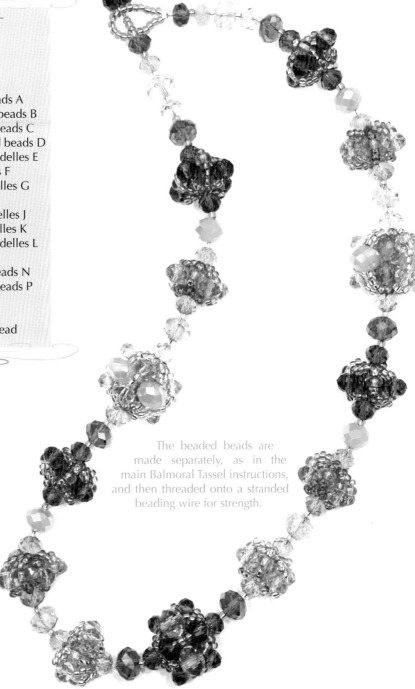

The beaded beads are made separately, as in the main Balmoral Tassel instructions, and then threaded onto a stranded beading wire for strength.

Following steps 20 and 21 make ten beaded beads in the following colours -

Make two with a colour combination of B, C, F, J, and P beads.
Make four with a colour combination of A, D, E, K and N beads.
Make four with a colour combination of A, C, H, L and N beads.

You also need to make three larger beaded beads.

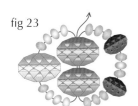

fig 23

Fig 23 shows the structure of the larger beaded bead.
Prepare the needle with 70cm of single thread and tie a keeper bead 10cm from the end.

Thread on 2F, 3C, 1A, 1G, 1A and 3C. Pass the needle through the 2F beads to bring the other nine beads into a strap around the side of the 2F. Thread on 3A, 1L, 1A, 1C, 1A, 1L and 3A. Pass the needle through the 2F beads to bring this new strap of eleven beads around the side of the 2F beads (fig 23).

As in steps 20 and 21 repeat these two straps three more times to give you eight alternating straps around the central 2F. Finish off the thread ends as before.

Repeat to make two more large beaded beads using 2F in the centre and B, C, E and J beads on the outside.

Starting at the centre front thread the beads onto the stranded beading wire in the order shown above. You may want to add more seed beads between the crystal beads towards the back of the design to make it a little longer. Save 1G for the clasp.

Thread one crimp onto one end of the wire followed by the 1G clasp bead, 1A and 3C. Pass the end of the wire back through the last 1A, 1G and the crimp (fig 24). Secure the crimp. At the other end of the wire thread on one crimp and 19A. Pass the end of the wire back through the crimp to form a loop and secure the crimp to finish off the design.

fig 24

Syon Tassel

You Will Need

Materials

3g of DB135 metallic midnight purple Delica beads A
4g of DB1340 silver lined bright fuchsia Delica beads B
1.5g of size 15/0 silver lined crystal seed beads C
4g of DB182 silver lined olive Delica beads D
4g of DB046 silver lined light green Delica beads E
1g of DB694 semi-matte silver lined purple Delica beads F
0.2g of DB002 metallic blue iris Delica beads G
0.1g of size 10/0 silver lined crystal seed beads H
Sixteen 4mm dark tanzanite crystal bicone beads J
Four 6x4mm tanzanite crystal rondelle beads K
Three 6x4mm emerald crystal rondelle beads L
One 8mm tanzanite crystal round bead M
One 20mm silver-plated solid hoop finding
A reel of purple size D beading thread
A reel of emerald size D beading thread

Tools

A size 13 beading needle
A pair of scissors to trim the threads

*The finished length of this tassel is 24cm
including the hanging loop.
It measures 21cm below the hanging loop.*

$\mathcal{F}$uchsias are such a staple of the garden that we forget how exotic & exquisite each individual bloom can be. With two contrasting colours layered over a clutch of dangling stamens they demand to be made into a tassel, earrings or a pendant.

The Tassel is Made in Six Stages
The three fuchsia flowers.
The fuchsia bud.
The large leaves.
The hoop assembly and decoration with small leaf motifs.
The butterfly.
The hanging loop.

1 The Fuchsia Flowers - The fuchsia flower has three distinct parts - the petals which form the tight trumpet; the sepals which curl outwards above the petal trumpet; and the stamens. The petals and the sepals are made separately from one another and then brought together as the stamens are created.

Prepare the needle with 1.2m of single purple thread and tie a keeper bead 15cm from the end.

2 The petals are supported on a ring of ladder-stitched beads. Thread on 4A. Pass the needle through the first 2A a second time to bring the four beads into a square (fig 1). Pass the needle up through the second 2A beads a second time (fig 2) and thread on 2A.

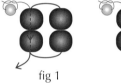

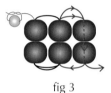

| fig 1 | fig 2 | fig 3 |

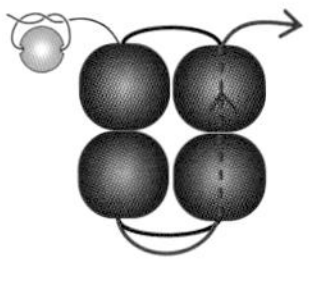

Pass the needle up through the second 2A once more to bring the new 2A alongside the second 2A. Pass the needle down through the new 2A (fig 3).

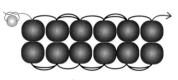
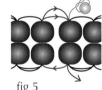

| fig 4 | fig 5 |

Repeat until you have six columns of 2A each (fig 4).

Bring the first column around to meet the last column and join the two together by passing the needle down the first, up the sixth and down the first (fig 5) to make a ring six beads in circumference and two beads deep.

3 Thread on 8A. Pass the needle back through the seventh A bead just added to bring the end A bead up as an anchor (fig 6).

Thread on 1A. Pass the needle back down the sixth A bead of the strand (fig 7).
Pass the needle up through the new A bead to bring it along-side the sixth A bead of the strand and thread on 1A.
Pass the needle down the fifth A bead on the first strand (fig 8).

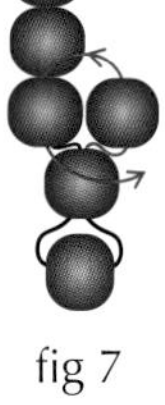

fig 6

fig 7

fig 8

4 Pass through the new A bead and thread on 1A. Attach this new A bead to the fourth A bead of the strand as before (fig 9).

Repeat three more times to add three new A beads alongside those of the first strand. Pass the needle up through the next column of 2A around the ring.

fig 9

To strengthen the petal pass the needle down through the 2A above the first strand and the first six A beads of the first strand.
Pass back up through the 6A just added and the 2A beads of the ring (fig 10).

fig 10

Pass the needle down through the next 2A of the ring and repeat steps 3 and 4 to make a second petal.

Repeat to make a third petal to complete the ring.

Finish off the thread ends neatly and securely.

5 The sepals are also supported on a ring of ladder-stitched beads, however this time the ring is three beads deep.

Prepare the needle with 1.5m of single purple thread and tie a keeper 15cm from the end. Thread on 6B.

Pass the needle down through the first 3B of the six and up through the second 3B (fig 11).

Thread on 3B and join it onto the second column of 3B as before.

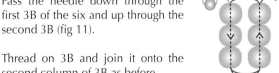

fig 11

Work until you have eight columns of three B beads each.

Join the last column to the first as in fig 5.

6 Thread on 8B. Pass the needle back through the seventh bead just added to bring the end B bead up as an anchor.

Thread on 6B and pass the needle up through the second column around the ring (fig 12). Pass the needle down through the column between the two strands and thread on 1B (fig 13).

This new bead needs to be attached to the B beads to each side of it.

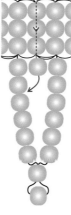

fig 12

fig 13

7 Pass the needle up through the first B bead of the first strand and down through the new B bead (fig 14).

Repeat with the top B bead of the second strand (fig 15).

fig 14

fig 15

fig 16

Thread on 1B and attach it to the B beads each side of it (the second B bead of the first strand and the fifth bead of the second strand) (see fig 16).

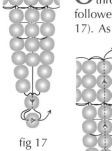

8 Thread on 2B. Pass the needle down through the 7th B bead of the first strand followed by the 8th B (the anchor bead) (fig 17). As you pull the thread the sepal will bend upwards as you have stretched 2B across a 4B gap.
Pass the needle back up through the 7th B bead, the 2B just added and the following 5B to emerge through the top of the column (fig 18).

fig 17

fig 18

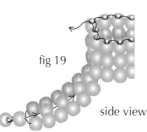

fig 19

side view

Pass the needle down the next column of 3B ready to make the next sepal.

Repeat from step 6 three times to complete four sepals in total.

9 The top edge of the ring now needs to be drawn in a little.
Thread on 1B. As you look down onto the top of the ring you can see the loops of thread between the holes in the beads.

Pass the needle under the second loop and back up through the new bead (fig 20) so that the new bead sits upright.

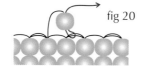

fig 20

10 Thread on 1B. Count two thread loops around the ring and repeat (fig 21).

fig 21

fig 22

Repeat the last stitch twice more. Pass the needle down the first B, underneath the thread loop and up through the B bead to complete a circle of 4B (fig 22).

Finish off the thread ends neatly and securely.

11 Prepare the needle as in step 1. Thread on 1B, 1J, 1B, 1A, and 1K. Pass the needle down through the holes in the centres of the ring of sepals and the ring of petals.

Thread on 1H, 30C, 1B, 1J, 1B and 3C. Leaving aside the last 3C beads to anchor the strand pass the needle back up through the last B bead threaded and the following J and B beads (fig 23).

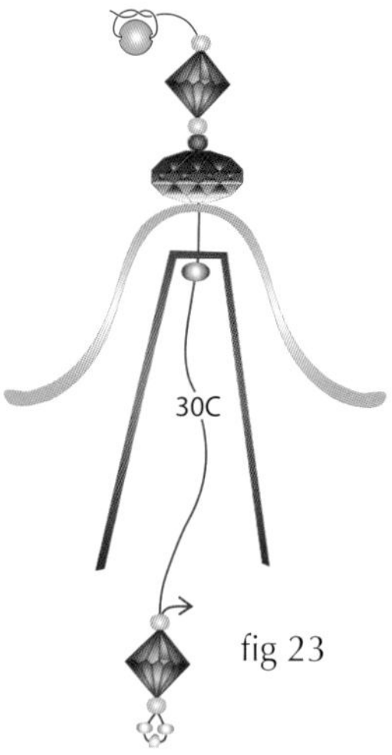

Pass the needle back up through the remainder of the strand to emerge through the very first B bead. Thread on 3A and pass the needle down through the beads above the sepals (fig 24).

Pass through the rings of sepals and petals and the single H bead to emerge at the top of the first stamen.

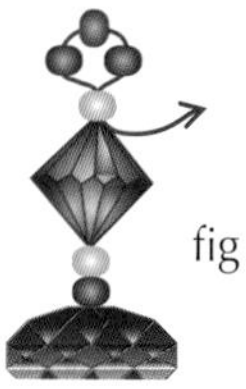

Thread on 20C, 1B, 1J, 1B and 3C for the second stamen. Make this stamen as before bringing the needle through to emerge at the keeper bead at the top of the work.

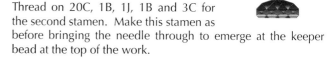

30C

fig 23

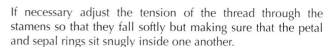

fig 24

If necessary adjust the tension of the thread through the stamens so that they fall softly but making sure that the petal and sepal rings sit snugly inside one another.

Finish off the thread ends neatly and securely.

Repeat from step 1 to make two more identical flowers.

12 The Fuchsia Bud - Repeat steps 1 to 4 inclusive using B beads instead of A beads. Do not finish off the thread end.

Following steps 9 and 10 add 3B beads along the top edge of the ring to draw the shape in a little.

13 Pass the needle down through the B beads of the first petal to emerge from the anchor bead at the bottom.
Pass the needle through the B beads at the bottom of the second and third petals.
Pass through the B bead at the bottom of the first petal again (fig 25) to link the three petal tips together.

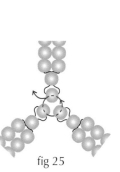

fig 25

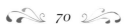

14
The bud needs to be tapered to a point. Thread on 3B. Pass the needle through the B bead on the bottom of the same petal and the 3B just added (fig 26).

Pass the needle through the 1B at the bottom of the next petal and thread on 1B. Pass the needle through the 1B at the tip of the work (fig 27).

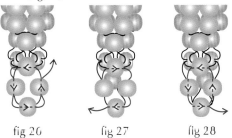

fig 26   fig 27   fig 28

Pass the needle up through the first 1B added in fig 26, the B bead at the bottom of the third petal, the B bead added in fig 27 and the B bead at the tip (fig 28).

Pass the needle through the beads of the closest petal to emerge from one of the 3B beads at the very top of the motif.

15
Pass the needle down the central hole of the ring so that it emerges between the petals and thread on 1K and 3A. Pass the needle back up through the K bead and out through the ring at the top of the motif to pull the 3A into a picot.

Pass the needle through one of the 3B beads at the top of the ring and back down the hole in the ring, the K bead and following 2A to emerge through the middle A bead. Referring to fig 29 stitch this bead to the ring of 3B created in fig 25 (fig 29). Pull quite firmly to make the petals curve around the K bead.

Pass the needle up through the third B bead of the picot, the K bead and the ring to emerge at the top of the motif.

fig 29

Remove the needle and set aside for the moment.

16
The Large Leaves - Prepare the needle with 1.2m of single emerald thread and tie a keeper bead 15cm from the end. Thread on 2D, 1L, and 17D.
Leaving aside the last 3D beads to anchor the strand pass the needle up through the 14th D bead (fig 30). Thread on 1D and pass the needle through the 3D beads of the anchor (fig 31).

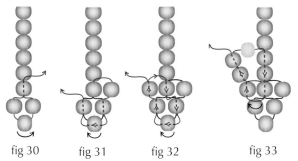

fig 30   fig 31   fig 32   fig 33

Thread on 1D. Pass the needle down through the 14th D bead, through the 3D beads of the anchor and up through the new 1D (fig 32).

Thread on 2D and 1E. Pass the needle down through the 12th, 13th and 14th D beads of the main strand and back up the last 3D beads added (fig 33).

17
Thread on 4D. Pass the needle down the 10th and 11th D beads of the main strand, the 1E added in the last stitch and up the first 2D of the 4D just added (fig 34).

fig 34

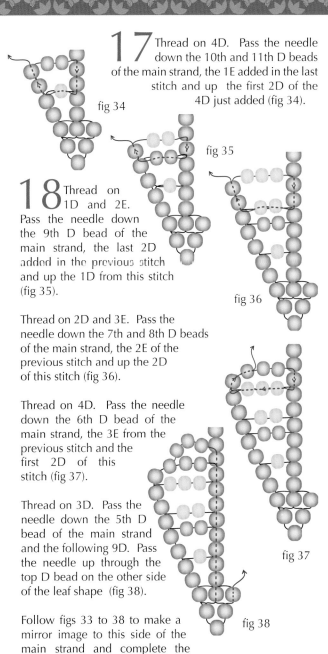

fig 35

18
Thread on 1D and 2E. Pass the needle down the 9th D bead of the main strand, the last 2D added in the previous stitch and up the 1D from this stitch (fig 35).

fig 36

Thread on 2D and 3E. Pass the needle down the 7th and 8th D beads of the main strand, the 2E of the previous stitch and up the 2D of this stitch (fig 36).

Thread on 4D. Pass the needle down the 6th D bead of the main strand, the 3E from the previous stitch and the first 2D of this stitch (fig 37).

Thread on 3D. Pass the needle down the 5th D bead of the main strand and the following 9D. Pass the needle up through the top D bead on the other side of the leaf shape (fig 38).

fig 37

Follow figs 33 to 38 to make a mirror image to this side of the main strand and complete the shaping.

fig 38

Pass the needle through the D beads around the edge of the leaf to make it a little more firm. Pass the needle up through the strand beads above the leaf to emerge alongside the keeper bead. Remove the needle and set aside for the moment.

Make a second leaf starting with 11D above the L bead.

Make a third and fourth leaf omitting the first 2D, 1L and 4D to make leaves with very short stems.

19

The Hoop - Prepare the needle with 1.5m of single emerald thread. Tie the end of the thread to the hoop with a double knot leaving a tail of 15cm.

Thread on 2D. Pass the needle through the centre of the hoop and in the opposite direction through the second D bead (fig 39). Adjust the thread tension so the two beads sit side by side on the outside edge of the hoop as shown.

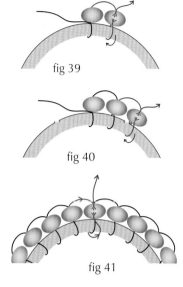

fig 39

fig 40

Thread on 1D. Pass the needle through the hoop and the new D bead in the opposite direction (fig 40).

Repeat the last stitch until the hoop has a complete circle of D beads around the edge. Link the last D bead to the first D bead as shown in fig 41.

fig 41

Remove the needle and allow the thread to fall loose - this will be the top of the hoop and the thread tail will give you a good reference point.

20

Prepare the needle with 1.5m of single emerald thread and attach to the beads at the bottom of the hoop to emerge immediately opposite the tail of thread from step 20.

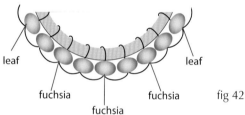

leaf   leaf

fuchsia   fuchsia   fig 42

fuchsia

Fig 42 shows the attachment positions of the three fuchsias and first two leaves. You need to create long green strands for the fuchsias to hang from.

The needle is emerging from the central D bead in fig 42. Thread on 50E, 1J, 7E, 1B, 1E, 1J, 1E, 1B, 3E, 1A, 1B, 1J, 1B, 1A and 2E. Pass the needle through the A bead at the very top of the first fuchsia flower and thread on 1E.
Pass the needle up through the first E bead of the 2E to pull the top of the fuchsia up close to the end of the strand (fig 43). Pass the needle up through the remaining beads of the strand and the D bead on the edge of the hoop.

fig 43

Pass the needle down the second D bead to the right around the hoop to be in the correct position to add the next fuchsia flower.

Thread on 12E, 1J, 7E, 1B, 1E, 1J, 1E, 1B, 3E, 1A, 1B, 1J, 1B, 1A and 2E. Pass the needle through the A bead at the top of the second fuchsia flower. Thread on 1E and complete the strand as before.

Reposition the needle to point outwards from the correct D bead ready to make the third fuchsia strand (see fig 42). Thread on 1E, 1B, 1J, 1B, 1A and 2E. Pass the needle through the top A bead of the third fuchsia and thread on 1E. Complete the strand as before.

21

Remove the needle from the working thread at the top of the third fuchsia strand and attach it to the loose thread end at the top of the first large leaf made. This leaf attaches to the hoop through the D bead to the left on fig 42 (closest to the shortest fuchsia). Pass the needle through the D bead indicated in fig 42, through the hoop, back through the same D bead on the hoop edge and down the D beads of the stem to the top of the leaf. Finish off the thread end neatly and securely.

Remove the keeper bead from this leaf and repeat the stitch through the D bead, the hoop and down into the leaf before securing in the same manner.

Repeat to add the second (longest) leaf to the remaining leaf bead position indicated on fig 42.

22

With reference to the photograph you will need to attach the remaining two leaves and the bud using the thread tails at the top of each of the motifs.

Attach the fuchsia bud to the front of the hoop above the longest fuchsia strand.
Attach the first leaf to the front of the hoop above the medium fuchsia strand pointing it to the right.
Attach the last leaf to the back of the hoop above the short fuchsia strand pointing it out to the other side in a similar fashion.

Leave the thread ends loose and attach the needle to the longest remaining end.

23

To finish off the beading you need to add a few clusters of D and E beads to conceal the attachment points of the larger motifs.

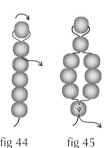

fig 44   fig 45

Bring the needle through one of the D beads on the hoop edge and thread on 6D. Pass the needle back through the fifth D (fig 44) and thread on 3D. Pass the needle through the first D bead to make a small leaf (fig 45).

Make a few of these leaves in both D and E beads and some smaller loops of 3D or 3E until you have created a pleasing cluster making the necessary concealments.

Finish off all of the thread ends neatly and securely.

24 The Butterfly - Prepare the needle with 1.5m of single purple thread and tie a keeper bead 15cm from the end.

Fig 46 shows the grid for the butterfly motif: it is worked in brick stitch. If you have not used this stitch before you will find additional instructions on page 10.

Make a ladder stitch foundation row along the 14 beads indicated on the grid.
Work up through the grid repositioning the needle through the beads of the pattern to make all of the necessary shaping. When you reach the first corner marked X on the top row you will need to add a small shaping stitch. The needle will be emerging from the top of the end A bead.

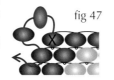

fig 46

A
B
F
G

← Start Here

Thread on 2A. Referring to fig 47 pass the needle down through the edge A bead of the previous row (fig 47).
Continue to complete the remainder of the grid adding a shaping stitch to the other X location.

fig 47

Leave the thread ends attached.
The hanging loop needs to be made before the final position for the butterfly can be decided.

25 The Hanging Loop - Re-attach the needle to the tail thread left at the end of step 19. Thread on 5D, 1M, 1D, 1B, 1D, 1A, 1L, 1A, 1D, 1B and 50D.

Referring to fig 48 pass the needle down through the last B bead threaded and thread on 1D.

Pass the needle through the next A bead and the following 1L and 1A.

Thread on 1D and pass the needle through the next 1B along.

Thread on 1D and pass the needle through the M bead (fig 48).

Pass the needle through the next 4D.

Hold the decoration up by the loop and assess how straight it is hanging. If the decoration applied to the bottom of the hoop is slightly wider to one side than the other the hoop will tip slightly.

fig 48

If the hoop is hanging well pass the needle through the last 1D of the beads added at the start of step 25 and through the D bead on the edge of the hoop.

If the hoop is tilting slightly to the side, thread on 1D and pass through the bead to the left or right on the edge of the hoop to compensate.

Pass the needle through the hoop and back up the beads added in step 25, around the loop and back down to the hoop. Repeat this thread path once more to make the loop strong.

Finish off the thread ends neatly and securely.

26 Offer the butterfly up to the hoop and stitch into place through the D beads around the hoop using the thread ends.

Finish off all remaining thread ends neatly and securely.

Syon Inspirations *Scissor Tassels*

Scissor tassels make a great present for someone who stitches for pleasure. They mark out their special scissors and say to others - don't use me for cutting paper or as a substitute for a screwdriver!

Butterfly Scissor Tassel

This is made using the same grid on page 73.

A is DB240
B is DB651
F is DB247
G is DB002

A tassel with a 6mm pinnk crystal bead at the top is made separately (see right).

A 4mm jump ring is stitched below the bottom G bead of the butterfly body to support the tassel.

A 4mm jump ring fits beautifully onto the space above the top H bead of the butterfly grid. It is held in place firmly with three stitches from the closest three beads (fig 49). An eyepin is used to link an 8mm amethyst crystal round to a further jump ring and a 10cm length of fine curb chain.

fig 49

The tassel is attached to the bottom of the butterfly with a 4mm jump ring. To allow the tassel to swing freely the tassel is not bound directly onto the ring but links to the ring via a loop of beads.

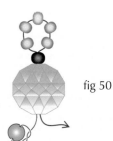

fig 50

Start the tassel thread with a keeper bead and pass the needle through a 6mm pink crystal. Thread on 1G and 5A. Pass the needle back through the 1G and the tassel top bead (fig 50) to be in the correct position to start the tassel stranding.

Make the tassel strands as desired. The needle needs to pass through the 1G and the loop of 5A above the tassel top bead after each strand to make the loop more firm.

Open the jump ring stitched to the base of the butterfly and link through the 5A loop.

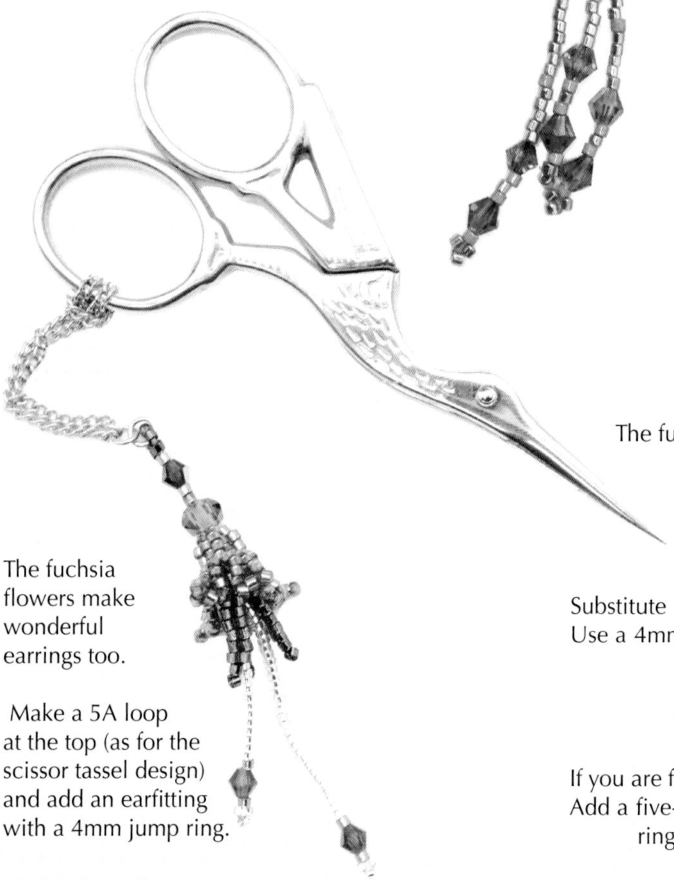

Fuchsia Scissor Tassel

The fuchsia flower drop is made following steps 1 to 11 in the Syon Tassel chapter.

A is DB1342
B is DB1338

Substitute 5A for the 3A used in fig 24 to make a slightly larger loop. Use a 4mm jump ring to link this 5A loop to a second 4mm jump ring and a 10cm length of fine curb chain.

Loop the chain through the handle of the scissors.

If you are feeling more ambitious make a leaf as in steps 16, 17 and 18. Add a five-bead loop to the top of the leaf stem and link it to the jump ring at the bottom of the chain with a separate jump ring.

The fuchsia flowers make wonderful earrings too.

Make a 5A loop at the top (as for the scissor tassel design) and add an earfitting with a 4mm jump ring.

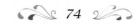

Bookmarks

Make an exquisite bookmark for a treasured book or a special gift.

Here a butterfly motif with a tassel has been used at the top and a copy of the same tassel has been attached to the bottom of the ribbon.

A is DB610
B is DB045
F is DB602
G is DB002

The motifs attach to either end of a length of ribbon using ribbon end clasps and 4mm jump rings.

Choose a double-satin ribbon as both sides of the ribbon show when the marker is in use.

Trim the cut end of the ribbon very neatly and place into the ribbon end clasp. Gently squeeze the clasp with a pair of flat-faced pliers to close. Make sure both edges of the clasp have gripped firmly onto the ribbon.

The blue and green bookmark was made from a a simple brick stitch grid with a five bead loop at the top and five fringe strands.

An 8mm crystal bead dangles from the other end of the ribbon.

You could design your own brick stitch motif or just add a simple tassel to each end of the ribbon.

Windsor Tassel

You Will Need

Materials

15g of size 10/0 black seed beads A
10g of size 10/0 lustre opaque chocolate seed beads B
8g of size 10/0 ceylon ivory seed beads C
8g of size 10/0 silver lined grey seed beads D
8g of size 6/0 metallic bronze AB seed beads E
4g of size 3 twisted black bugle beads F
Thirty 6x4mm Colorado topaz crystal rondelles G
Nine 6x4mm black crystal rondelles H
Nineteen 6x4mm metallic bronze crystal rondelles J
Five 8x6mm Colorado topaz crystal rondelles K
Six 8x6mm black crystal rondelles L
Twenty-two 8x6mm metallic bronze crystal rondelles M
Two 8mm Colorado topaz crystal rounds N
Seventeen 8mm black crystal rounds P
Two 8mm metallic bronze crystal rounds Q
One 30mm round wooden base bead
30cm of stranded beading wire
Two gilt French crimps
A reel of black size D beading thread
A piece of paper approximately 40x100mm in size

Tools

A size 10 beading needle
A pair of scissors to trim the threads
A pair of flat-faced pliers or crimping pliers

*The finished length of this tassel is 29cm
including the hanging loop.
It measures 24cm below the hanging loop.*

Luxurious, sumptuous and fit for a castle this tassel demands to be threaded onto a silky twisted rope and cinched around a thickly-lined brocade curtain or as a glamorous decoration for the key to a grand boudoir.

The Tassel is Made in Five Stages

The large base bead is covered with a beaded net pattern.
The tassel stranding below the large bead is worked.
The small rondelle-shaped beaded bead above the large decorated bead is made.
The tassel strands are pulled up below the large decorated bead and the design assembled to just below the strap.
The hanging strap is made and attached to the top of the tassel.

1 The Large Base Bead - You will be using all of the different types and colours of the beads listed except for the bugle beads F to make the netted covering for the wooden base bead. You will find it useful to lay out and label the beads clearly before you start.

The netting is supported on a series of beaded straps that pass top to bottom over the large bead: as the pattern develops you will see the sequence of six toning stripes that spiral around the bead start to appear. Each colour of crystal bead is paired with a seed bead colour to make the spiral effect more defined.

A is the background colour
B is paired with G, K and N
C is paired with H, L and P
D is paired with J, M and Q

The paired seed bead colours make diamond-shaped frames around the crystal beads.

Look ahead to fig 15 to see how the bead pairings form the spiral pattern.

Examine the large wooden bead - you may be able to see small wooden fibres pushing into the hole and around the edges of the hole - it is important that the hole is smooth. Push a knitting needle, or similar, through the hole to smooth the fibres.

Taking the 40x100mm piece of paper and referring to Step 1 in the Balmoral Tassel chapter (page 63), line the hole in the wooden bead. Prepare the needle with 2m of single thread and attach firmly to the paper tube. Pass the needle through the wooden bead ready to start the netting. This bead will now be referred to as the large base bead.

Extra Info....

When you need a new thread length start it with a double stitch through the paper - leave the old end hanging loose as you don't want to block the bead holes with knots. When the beading is complete carefully undo these double stitches and tie the thread ends together in pairs with a secure double knot. Pass each end through a few beads to neaten and trim.

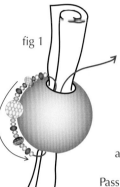

fig 1

2 Thread on 1A, 1F, 1A, 1B, 1G, 1B, 1A, 1E, 1A, 1C, 1P, 1C, 1A, 1E, 1A, 1D, 1J, 1D, 1A, 1E and 1A.

Pass the needle through the large base bead to make a strap around the side (fig 1).

*Thread on 5A, 1E, 1A, 1B, 1K, 1B, 1A, 1E, 1A, 1C, 1L, 1C, 1A, 1E and 5A.

Pass the needle through the large base bead to make a second strap alongside the first one (fig 2).

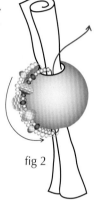

fig 2

For simplicity figs 3 to 14 will show the two straps lying parallel to one another - on your work the straps will come closer together at the top and bottom.

fig 3

3 Pass the needle through the first six beads of the strap just made to emerge from the first E bead of the strap (fig 3).

To create the netted effect the E beads from this strap will be linked across to the crystal beads on the previous strap and vice versa.

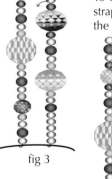

fig 4

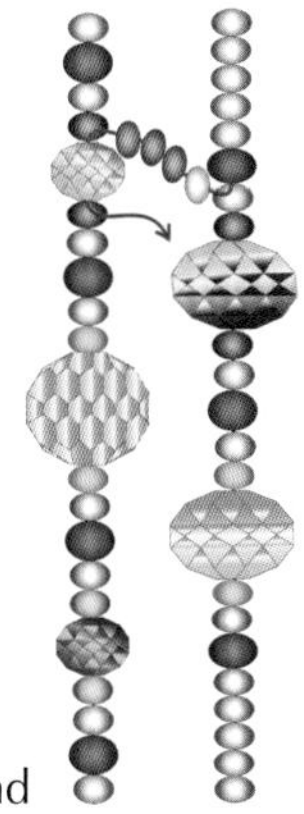

4 Thread on 1A and 3B. Pass the needle through the 1G bead on the previous strap (fig 4).

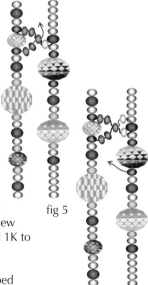

fig 5

5 Thread on 2B and pass the needle through the first of the 3B beads in the opposite direction (fig 5).

Thread on 1A and pass the needle through the first E bead of the new strap and the following 1A, 1B and 1K to emerge from the K bead (fig 6).

This creates half of a diamond-shaped frame around the first G bead on the first strap and repositions the needle for the next stitch.

fig 6

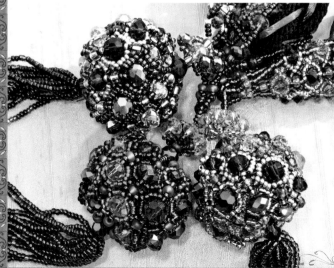

6

The K bead needs to link across to the next E bead on the previous strap.

Thread on 4B and 1A. Pass the needle through the E bead on the previous strap (fig 7).

Thread on 1A and pass the needle through the last B bead of the 4B in the opposite direction and thread on 3B. Pass the needle through the K bead on the new strap and the following 1B, 1A and 1E (fig 8).

fig 7   fig 8

This creates half of a diamond-shaped frame around the K bead - note how the B bead count increased to make the frame fit around the larger bead.

7

The E bead now needs to link across to the P bead on the first strap.

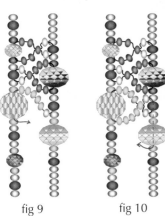

Thread on 1A and 5C. Pass the needle through the P bead (fig 9).

Thread on 4C and pass the needle through the first 1C of the 5C beads in the opposite direction.

Thread on 1A and pass the needle through the E bead on the second strap and the following 1A, 1C and 1L (fig 10).

fig 9   fig 10

This creates half of a diamond-shaped frame around the P bead on the first strap and repositions the needle for the next stitch. Again note that the bead count has changed to fit around the larger bead - you have also swapped to the C bead colour which is paired with the P bead colour.

8

The L bead now needs to link across to the E bead on the previous strap.

Thread on 4C and 1A. Pass the needle through the E bead on the previous strand and thread on 1A.

Pass the needle through the last C bead of the 4C just added in the opposite direction and thread on 3C.

Pass the needle through the L bead and the following 1C, 1A and 1E on the new strap (fig 11).

fig 11

This completes half of a diamond-shaped frame around the L bead on the second strap and repositions the needle for the next stitch. Note that the C bead count has dropped to fit around the slightly smaller crystal bead.

The E bead now needs to link across to the J bead on the first strap.

9

Thread on 1A and 3D. Pass the needle through the J bead and thread on 2D.

Pass the needle through the first D bead of the 3D just added in the opposite direction and thread on 1A.

Pass the needle through the E bead and the following 5A on the second strap to emerge from the bottom bead of the strap (fig 12).

Note that the bead count on this link has dropped again to accomodate the smallest size crystal bead but, throughout the links, the A bead count has remained the same.   fig 12

Pass the needle through the large base bead.

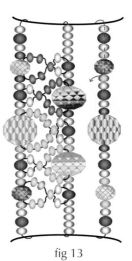

10

For the next strap thread on 1A, 1E, 1A, 1D, 1J, 1D, 1A, 1E, 1A, 1B, 1N, 1B, 1A, 1E, 1A, 1C, 1H, 1C, 1A, 1E and 1A. Pass the needle through the large base bead to draw the new strap alongside the previous strap.

Pass the needle through the first 1A, 1E, 1A, 1D and 1J beads of the new strap (fig 13).

You are now in the correct position to start the links between the crystals and E beads of the new strap and those of the previous strap.

fig 13

For the next set of links follow fig 14 throughout.

11

The first link connects to the J bead so you need to work in D beads.

Thread on 3D and 1A. Pass the needle through the E bead on the previous strap and thread on 1A. Pass the needle through the last 1D bead threaded and thread on 2D.

Pass the needle through the J bead on the new strap and the following 1D, 1A and 1E ready to make the next link.

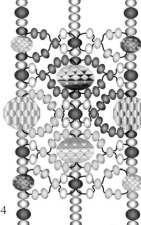

fig 14

The next link connects to a K bead so you will need to work in B beads.

Thread on 1A and 4B. Pass the needle through the K bead on the previous strap and thread on 3B. Pass the needle through the first of the 4B beads and thread on 1A.

Pass the needle through the E bead on the new strap and the following 1A, 1B and 1N ready to make the next link.

Note that you have completed a diamond-shaped frame around the K bead.

14 Pass the needle through the first 5A and 1E of the new strap ready to start the first link between this E bead and the top crystal bead of the previous strap (see fig 3).

Make the links between this new strap and the previous strap as in figs 4 - 12 inclusive swapping the seed bead colours as appropriate to match the crystal beads along the straps thus -

Work a link as in figs 4 - 6 with D beads.
A link as in fig 7 - 8 with D beads.
A link as in figs 9 - 10 with B beads.
A link as in fig 11 with B beads.
A link as in fig 12 with C beads (see fig 15).

Pass the needle through the large base bead ready to make the next strap.

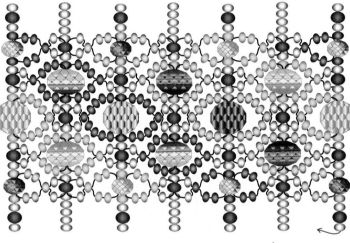

fig 15

Referring to fig 15 thread up the fifth strap -
1A, 1E, 1A, 1C, 1H, 1C, 1A, 1E, 1A, 1D, 1Q, 1D, 1A, 1E, 1A, 1B, 1G, 1B, 1A, 1E and 1A. Pass the needle through the large base bead.

Pass the needle through the first 1A, 1E, 1A, 1C and 1H of the new strap ready to make the first link (see fig 15).

Following figs 14 and 15 -
Make the first link with C beads.
Make next two links with D beads.
Make the last two links with B beads (see fig 15).

Pass the needle through the large base bead ready to make the next strap.

Referring to fig 15 thread up the sixth strap with 5A, 1E, 1A, 1C, 1L, 1C, 1A, 1E, 1A, 1D, 1M, 1D, 1A, 1E and 5A. Pass the needle through the large base bead.

Pass the needle through the first 5A and 1E ready to make the first link (as fig 3).

Referring to fig 15 -
Make the first two links with C beads.
Make the next two links with D beads.
Make the last link with B beads **.

Pass the needle through the large base bead ready to make the next strap.

15 The seventh strap is a repeat of the first strap - thread on 1A, 1E, 1A, 1B, 1G, 1B, 1A, 1E, 1A, 1C, 1P, 1C, 1A, 1E, 1A, 1D, 1J, 1D, 1A, 1E and 1A (see fig 15).

Pass the needle through the large base bead and the first 1A, 1E, 1A, 1B and 1G of the new strap ready to make the first link.

12 The next link connects to an N bead so you will need to work in B beads.
Thread on 5B and 1A. Pass the needle through the E bead on the previous strap and thread on 1A. Pass the needle through the last B bead of the 5B just added and thread on 4B. Pass the needle through the N bead and the following 1B, 1A and 1E ready to make the next link.

The next link connects to an L bead so you will need to work in C beads.
Thread on 1A and 4C. Pass the needle through the L bead on the previous strap and thread on 3C. Pass the needle through the first of the 4C beads and thread on 1A. Pass the needle through the E bead on the new strap and the following 1A, 1C and 1H ready to make the next link.
Note that you have completed a diamond-shaped frame around the L bead.

The last link connects to an H bead so you will need to work in C beads.
Thread on 3C and 1A. Pass the needle through the E bead on the previous strap and thread on 1A. Pass the needle through the last 1C bead threaded and thread on 2C. Pass the needle through the H bead on the new strap and the following 1C, 1A, 1E and 1A to emerge at the bottom of the strap (fig 14).

Pass the needle through the large base bead.

13 For the fourth strap - thread on 5A, 1E, 1A, 1D, 1M, 1D, 1A, 1E, 1A, 1B, 1K, 1B, 1A, 1E and 5A. Pass the needle through the large base bead to draw the new strap up alongside the previous strap.

16

Referring to fig 15 -
Make the first link with B beads.
The next two links with C beads.
The last two links with D beads.

Pass the needle through the large base bead ready to make the next strap.

Referring to fig 15 and your work you can see that the first strap and the last strap are identical. Return to the * in step 2 and repeat to the ** in step 14 to make a further five straps with their associated links. Pass the needle through the large base bead in readiness for the final set of links.

17

To complete the netted pattern you now need to link the last strap worked to the first strap.

Pass the needle through the first 1A, 1E, 1A, 1B and 1G of the very first strap to be in the correct position for the link.

Following the last set of links on fig 15 join the first strap made to the last one made. Pass the needle through the large base bead.

Although the beaded pattern is now complete it can be a little distorted where the larger crystal beads push against the large base bead. The diamond-shaped frames are now joined together along the diagonals to make the whole net come together more firmly.

18

The sides of adjacent frames are linked together with a simple square stitch (see fig 16). The needle is then repositioned through the beads of the next strap and the link repeated (see fig 17). Figs 17 and 18 show the beads in bold along the frame edges that need to be linked together along one diagonal.

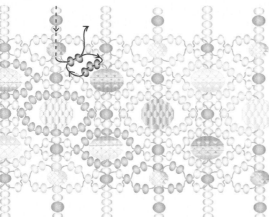

fig 16

Following fig 16 choose a strap with a G, H or J bead at the top. Pass the needle through the first five beads of the strap and the first two beads of the diamond frame. These two beads need to be stitched to the three beads of the slightly larger frame lying adjacent. Pass the needle through the three beads along the side of this frame and the two beads on the first frame again to make a square stitch (fig 16).

19

Referring to fig 17 pass the needle through the following two seed beads before the E bead on the next strap. Pass down through this E bead, the following three beads of this strap and the middle two beads of the next diamond-shaped frame as shown (fig 17).
Make a square stitch to join these three frame beads to the middle two highlighted frame beads around the large crystal.

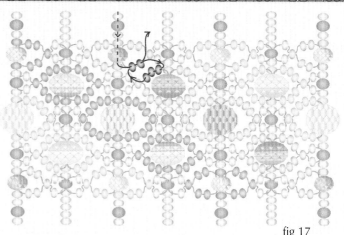

fig 17

20

Following fig 18 pass the needle up to and through the beads of the next strap to emerge from the large crystal bead. Pass through the first three beads of this frame and square stitch the middle two beads of this frame edge to the three frame beads of the next crystal along the diagonal (fig 18).

Reposition the needle again following fig 18 and make the final square stitch of the diagonal. Pass the needle through to emerge from the bottom bead of the next strap along (fig 18). Pass the needle through the large base bead.

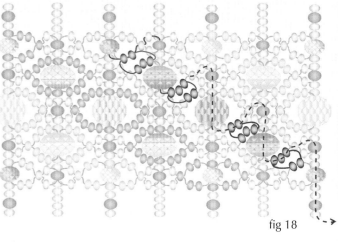

fig 18

Repeat steps 18, 19 and 20 starting at the top of the next strap with a G, H or J bead at the top.

Repeat until the six diagonals are all square stitched together.

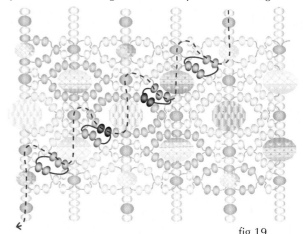

fig 19

21

You now need to square stitch the diagonals in the opposite direction (fig 19). Work all six diagonals in the in the same manner as before.

Finish off the thread ends but do not remove the paper tube.

22
The Tassel Stranding - This is made as a separate unit with a P bead at the top - the P bead is then pulled into place during final assembly.

Prepare the needle with 2m of single thread.
Tip out your E beads and choose one bead with a larger than average hole.
Tip out your P beads and choose the bead with the largest hole size - this will be the bead that you use at the top of the tassel.
Tie the selected E bead to the thread 15cm from the end with a secure double knot and thread on the tassel top P bead - these two beads form the top of the tassel.

Thread on 20A, 2D, 3A, 2D, 1C, 2D, 1A, 2D, 2C, 1B, 1E, 1B, 2C, 1F, 1A, 1F, 1C, 1F, 1D, 1C, 1D, 1F, 1D, 1B, 1E, 1B, 1G, 1D, 1F, 1D, 1E, 1D, 1A, 1M, 1A, 1E, 1D, 1A, 1E, 1A, 1E, 1C, 1P, 1C, 1D, 1J, 1A, 1E, 1A, 1B and 15A.

Leaving aside the last 15A beads threaded to anchor the strand pass the needle up through the last B bead threaded and the following 11 beads to emerge from the middle E bead above the P bead (fig 20).

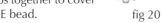

This E bead is now embellished with straps of A, B, C and D beads.

Thread on 5A. Pass the needle through the E bead again to bring the A beads into a strap around the side of the E bead (fig 21).

Repeat to make a strap of 5B, a strap of 5C and a strap of 5D beads.

fig 21

Push these straps together to cover one half of the E bead.

fig 20

Now repeat the four straps, in the same sequence, to give you eight alternating colour straps in total.

Pass the needle through the A bead on the main strand above the embellished E bead and the following beads of the strand to emerge from the P bead at the very top.

Pass the needle through the E bead above the P bead and back down the P bead ready to make the next tassel strand (fig 22).

Make the second tassel strand as for the first.   fig 22

Repeat until you have thirteen tassel strands in total. Finish off the thread ends neatly and securely.

23
The Beaded Rondelle - Prepare the needle with 1.5m of single thread and tie a keeper bead 15cm from the end.

Thread on 1M, 2D, 1B, 1G, 1B and 2D. Pass the needle through the M bead to bring the other beads into a strap to the side of the larger bead (fig 23).

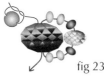

fig 23

Thread on 2D, 1B, 1G, 1B and 2D. Pass the needle through the M bead to create a second strap.

Repeat until you have seven straps in total - this will completely cover the M bead. Remove the keeper bead and finish off both thread ends without blocking the hole in the M bead.

24
Assembling the Tassel - Remove the paper tube from the large decorated bead, select the H bead with the largest hole and six A beads with generous hole sizes.

Thread the E bead at the top of the tassel strands onto the centre of the stranded beading wire. Bring the two ends of the wire together and pass through the large decorated bead, 1P, 1E, the beaded rondelle made in step 23 and 1E. Push the components up close together so the P bead at the top of the tassel strands and the new P bead nestle down snugly into the holes at either end of the large decorated bead.

Separate the two wire ends and onto each end thread three of the reserved 6A and 1 French crimp.

Pass the two ends of the wire in opposite directions through the larger-holed H bead, the crimps and the A beads just added (it will be a tight squeeze to fit the wire through the A beads) (fig 24).   fig 24

Pull everything up tightly and squash the crimps flat to grip the wire with a pair of flat pliers or similar.

Carefully trim away the excess wire.

25 The Hanging Strap - The hanging strap is made separately from the main tassel and then firmly attached to the H bead at the top of the tassel arrangement.

Prepare the needle with 1.5m of single thread and tie a keeper bead 15cm from the end.

Thread on 1E, 2A, 1E, 1A, 1E, 1A, 1E and 1A. Pass the needle through the first 1A and 1E beads in the opposite direction to make a tag-shaped loop (fig 25).

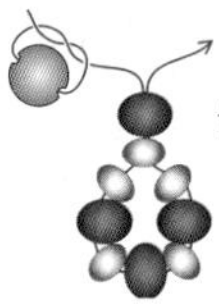

 fig 25

Thread on 1A, 1B, 1G, 1B, 1A, 1E, 1A, 1D, 1J, 1D, 1A, 1E, 1A, 1C, 1L, 1C, 1A, 1E, 1A, 1B, 1K, 1B, 1A, 1E, 1A, 1C, 1L, 1C, 1A, 1E, 1A, 1D, 1J, 1D, 1A, 1E, 1A, 1B, 1G, 1B, 1A, 1E, 2A, 1E, 1A, 1E, 1A, 1E and 1A.

Following fig 26 pass the needle through the first 1A of the 2A beads just threaded and the following 1E, 1A, 1B and 1G beads to pull this end of the row into a matching loop (fig 26).

26 Thread on 5B, 1A and 1B. Leaving aside the last three beads threaded to form a picot pass the needle back through the fourth B bead just added in the opposite direction.

fig 26

Thread on 3B and pass through the G bead on the main strand in the same direction as before (fig 27) to create half of a diamond-shaped frame.

 fig 27   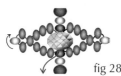 fig 28

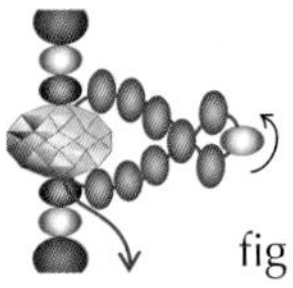

Repeat step 26 to make the second half of the frame to the other side of the G bead (fig 28).

Pass the needle through the following three beads of the main strand to emerge from the next E bead.

27 Thread on 1A, 4C, 1H and 3C. Pass the needle in the opposite direction through the first C bead to draw the crystal bead up into a loop. Thread on 1A and pass the needle through the 1E bead on the main strand in the same direction as before (fig 29).

fig 29

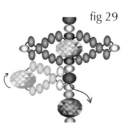

Repeat step 27 to make a matching loop to the other side of the same E bead.

Pass the needle through the following three beads of the main strap to emerge from the J bead.

28 Following figs 27 and 28 make a similar diamond-shaped frame around the J bead but using D beads instead of B beads.

Pass the needle through the following three beads on the main strand to emerge from the next E bead.

Repeat step 27 to make a second pair of crystal loops from this E bead using the B seed beads and a G crystal bead.

Pass the needle through the next 3 beads of the main strand to emerge from the L bead.

29 Thread on 6C, 1A and 1C. Leaving aside the last three beads threaded to form a picot pass the needle back through the fifth C bead just added in the opposite direction.

Thread on 4C and pass through the L bead on the main strand in the same direction as before (see fig 30) to create half of a diamond-shaped frame.

Repeat step 29 to make the second half of the frame to the other side of the L bead (fig 30).

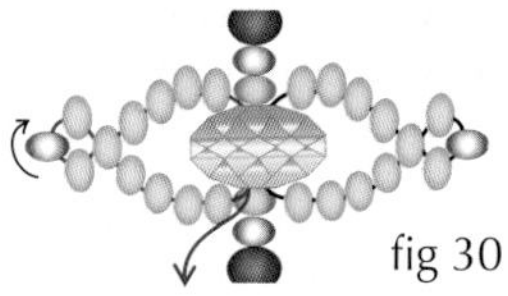

 fig 30

Pass the needle through the following 3 beads of the main strand to emerge from the next E bead.

30 Thread on 1A, 5D, 1M and 4D. Pass the needle through the first of the 5D beads in the opposite direction and thread on 1A.

Pass the needle through the E bead on the main strand to make a slightly longer crystal loop than before (fig 31).

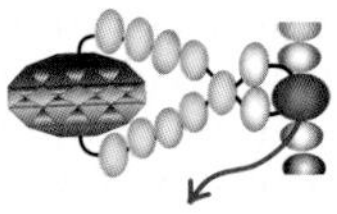

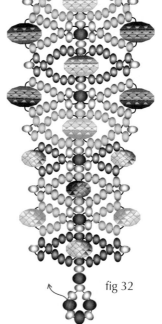

fig 31

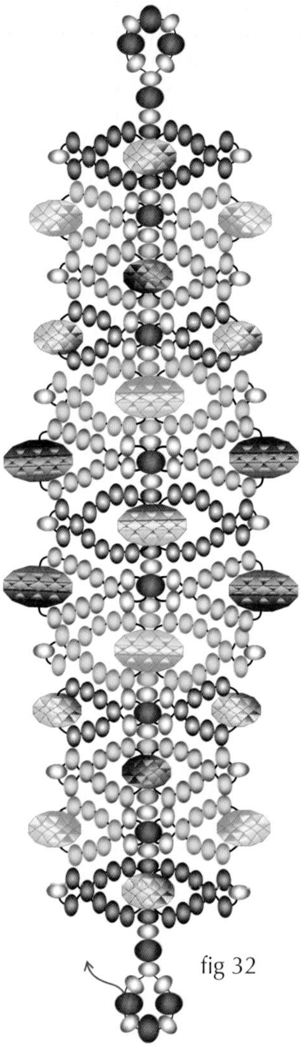

Repeat to make an identical loop on the other side of the E bead.

Pass the needle through the next three beads of the main strand to emerge from the K bead.

Repeat fig 30 using B beads instead of C beads.

You are now at the centre of the strap.

Referring to fig 32 work towards the other end of the main strand making the diamond-shaped frames and crystal loops to match those already made.

Pass the needle through the beads of the end tag to emerge from the third E bead of the tag pointing towards the main length of the strap (fig 32).

You now need to link up the A beads at the tips of the diamond-shaped frames with the crystal beads at the ends of the crystal loops.

fig 32

31

Referring to fig 33 throughout thread on 7A. Pass the needle through the A bead at the tip of the first diamond-shaped frame.

Thread on 2A and 1C. Pass through the H bead at the end of the adjacent crystal loop.

Thread on 1C and 2A. Pass through the next A bead tip.

Thread on 2A and 1B. Pass through the G bead.

Thread on 1B and 2A. Pass through the next A bead tip.

Thread on 2A and 1D. Pass through the M bead.

Thread on 1D and 2A. Pass through the next A bead tip.

You are now at the centre of the sequence - work the remainder of this edge as a mirror image.

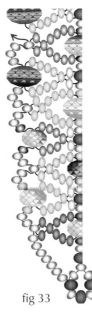

fig 33

Windsor Inspirations
Eton Bracelet

The hanging strap easily adapts into a bracelet design. Just add a bead and loop clasp to either end.

This example uses the smaller 6x4mm rondelles throughout giving a delicate touch to the design.

32

Pass the needle through the beads of the end tag and repeat step 30 through the crystals and A bead tips at the other side of the strap.

Pass the needle through these edge sequences once more to make the work more firm.

Bring the needle through to emerge from the E bead at the tip of one end of the strap.

33

Thread on 3A. Pass the needle through the H bead at the top of the tassel assembly. Thread on 3A and pass the needle through the E bead at the end of the strap once more (fig 34). Pass the needle through this connection twice more.

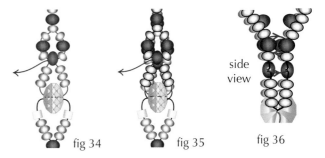

fig 34　　　fig 35　　side view　fig 36

Pass the needle through to emerge from the H bead.

Bring up the other end of the strap and make two 3A bead connections between the E bead at the tip of this strap end and the H bead (fig 35). Reinforce the link with two more passes of the needle.

34

To make the strap connection stay firm you will need to stitch the two strap ends together through the E beads. Referring to fig 36 stitch through the corresponding E beads on the two strap ends twice to bring the strap ends together just above the H bead.

If the needle will fit through the H bead again reinforce the join between the bottom E beads and the H bead until the needle will not pass through again. Finish off the thread ends neatly and securely.

Babushka Tassel

You Will Need

Materials

7g of size 10/0 purple scarab seed beads A
4g of size 10/0 transparent purple AB seed beads B
4g of size 10/0 silver lined magenta seed beads C
12g of size 3 purple scarab twisted bugle beads D
12g of size 3 silver lined purple AB bugle beads E
10g of size 3 silver lined magenta bugle beads F
Two 18mm purple glass beads with a large (3-5mm) hole G
One 8mm purple fire polished faceted glass bead H
Twenty-seven 4mm purple AB fire polished faceted glass beads J
Four 6mm purple AB fire polished faceted glass beads K
One 12mm purple fire polished faceted glass bead L
One 4mm silver plated jump ring
50cm of stranded beading wire
Two black French crimps
A reel of black size D beading thread
Two pieces of paper approximately 30x80mm in size

Tools

A size 10 beading needle
A pair of scissors to trim the threads
A pair of flat-faced pliers or crimping pliers

The finished length of this tassel is 22cm including the hanging loop.

The texture and play of light on fur holds a deep fascination & cruelty-free artifical fur give us all the opportunity to look like Russian royalty. Interpreting this spikey but soft texture in beads means that everyone wants to touch this tassel.

The Tassel is Made in Five Stages

The first G bead is covered with a tightly-fitted skin of A beads.

The long tassel strands are worked outwards from the A beads covering the G bead.

A separate, slim tassel is made for the bottom of the design to form a tapered point.

The second G bead is covered with a lattice of seed beads and faceted glass beads.

The three separate parts are brought together with the remaining faceted beads to assemble the final design and add the hanging loop.

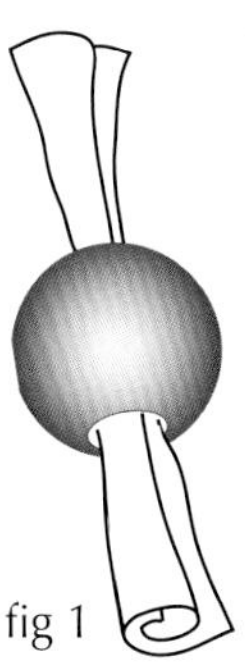

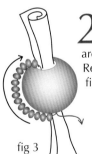

1 The First G Bead - To create a beaded decoration over the surface you will need to pass the needle through the hole in the large bead many times. To prevent the small beads from 'falling into' the hole of the large bead you need to restrict its diameter.

Take the 30x80mm piece of paper and roll it lengthwise to make a long slim tube. Push the tube into the G bead so that it sits in the centre of the length (fig 1).

fig 1

The needle will pass through the bead between the wall of the hole and the outer surface of the paper roll. Make sure you do not pierce the paper as you pass through the bead. Try to make the stitches through the bead as vertical as possible so the thread will pull straight through the large bead.

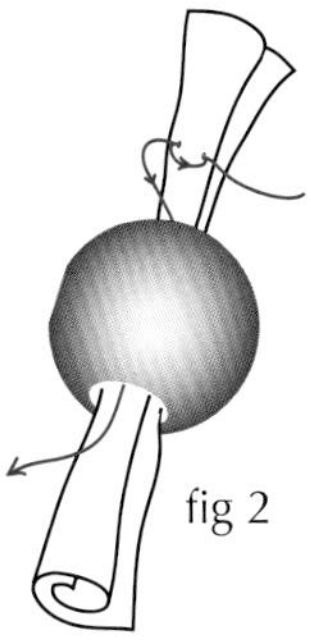

Prepare the needle with 1.5m of single thread.

Make a double stitch through the paper roll 15cm from the end of the thread to make an anchor. Pass the needle through the G bead (fig 2).

fig 2

2 Thread on 15A. Pass the needle through the G bead to draw the 15A up into a strap around the large bead (fig 3).
Repeat this stitch four more times to give you five straps of 15 A in total.

Referring to fig 4 pass the needle through the first 4A of the last strap worked. Thread on 7A.

fig 3

Pass the needle through the last 4A of this same strap and through the G bead (fig 4) to bring this small strap alongside the previous strap. This small strap will help to 'fill-out' the covering.

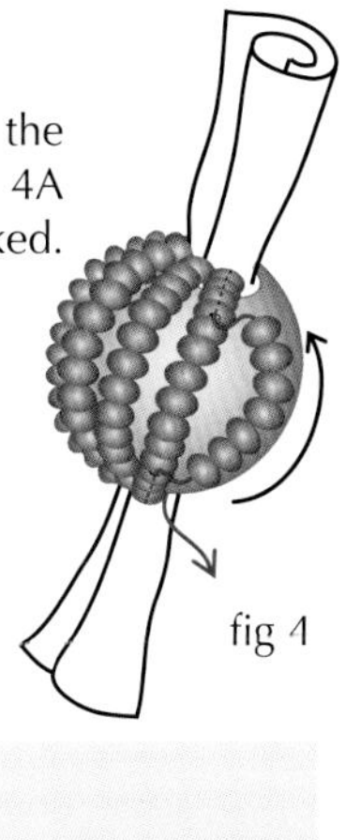

fig 4

Extra Info....
For a smoother alternative to the rolled paper tube try using a plastic straw to fill the hole in the G bead - if necessary slit the straw from top to bottom to make it a little slimmer to slide into the bead.

3 Repeat step 2 three more times around the G bead to complete twenty straps of 15A with four short straps of 7A in total. The G bead should now be quite well covered with A beads.

You will be starting the tassel strands next. You need to make sure that you have sufficient thread length for each tassel strand before you work it. If your thread measures 25cm or less, start a new 1.5m thread length now.

4 The Tassel Strands - Each 15A row of beads covering the G bead will have tassel strands attached to it - the short 7A sections do not support any tassel strands so you will need to skip past them as you proceed. Each row of 15A is worked in turn. You start at the bottom of the G bead with the longest tassel strand making the subsequent strands shorter and shorter until you reach the shortest strand that attaches to the top A bead of the row.

For clarity the diagrams for the following steps show just one row of 15A at a time.

Pass the needle through the first 1A bead of the closest row of 15A (fig 5).

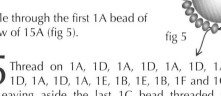

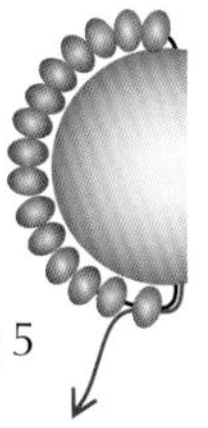

fig 5

5 Thread on 1A, 1D, 1A, 1D, 1A, 1D, 1A, 1D, 1A, 1D, 1A, 1E, 1B, 1E, 1B, 1F and 1C. Leaving aside the last 1C bead threaded to anchor the strand pass the needle up through the beads just added to emerge alongside the A bead of the 15A row (fig 6).

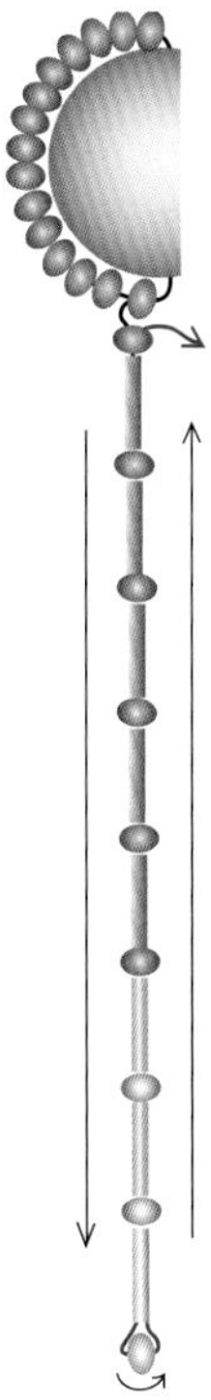

Carefully adjust the tension in the strand - the beads need to touch one another but fall softly from the top of the strand. As the strand contains a lot of bugle beads it can distort if you pull the thread too tightly - you will need to leave about 1mm of thread showing at the top of the strand.

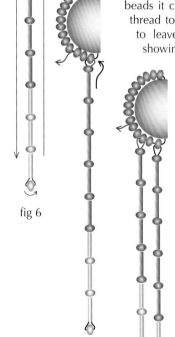

Pass the needle through the 1A bead on the 15A row in the same direction as before and the following 2A (fig 7). Check the tension in the strand again.

fig 6

For the next strand thread on 1A, 1D, 1A, 1D, 1A, 1D, 1A, 1D, 1A, 1E, 1B, 1E, 1B, 1F and 1C. Complete the strand as before passing the needle through the 1A on the 15A row at the top of the strand and the following 2A (fig 8).

fig 7

Check the tension in the strand just completed.

fig 8

6 So far you have two tassel strands attached to the first and third A beads of the row of 15A. The needle is emerging from the fifth A bead of the 15A.

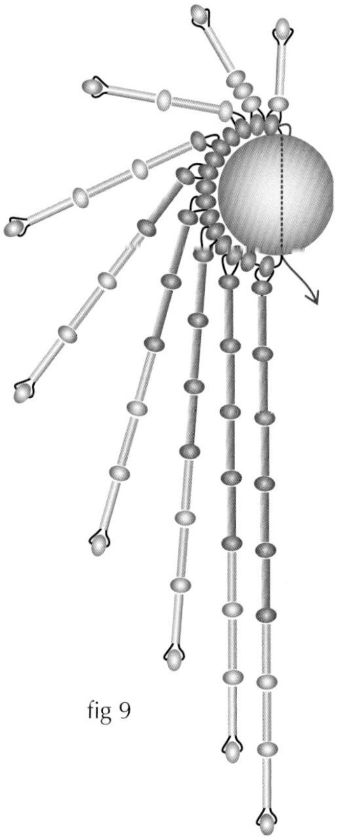

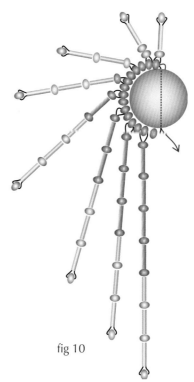

Referring to fig 9 throughout -

Make the third strand here from 1A, 1D, 1A, 1D, 1A, 1D, 1A, 1E, 1B, 1E, 1B, 1F and 1C. Pass the needle through the fifth A bead of the 15A row at the top of the strand and the following 2A to emerge from the seventh A bead of the 15A row.

Make the fourth strand here from 1A, 1D, 1A, 1D, 1A, 1E, 1B, 1E, 1B, 1F and 1C. Pass the needle through the seventh A bead of the 15A row at the top of the strand and the following 2A to emerge from the ninth A bead of the 15A row.

fig 9

Make the fifth strand here from 1A, 1D, 1A, 1E, 1B, 1E, 1B, 1F and 1C. Pass the needle through the ninth A bead of the 15A row at the top of the strand and the following 2A to emerge from the eleventh A bead of the 15A row.

Make the sixth strand here from 1A, 1E, 1B, 1E, 1B, 1F and 1C. Pass the needle through the eleventh A bead of the 15A row at the top of the strand and the following 2A to emerge from the thirteenth A bead of the 15A row.

Make the seventh strand here from 1B, 1E, 1B, 1F and 1C. Pass the needle through the thirteenth A bead of the 15A row at the top of the strand and the following 1A to emerge from the fourteenth A bead of the 15A row.

Make the eighth strand here from 3B, 1F and 1C. Pass the needle through the fourteenth A bead of the 15A row at the top of the strand and the following 1A to emerge from the last A bead of the 15A row. Pull the thread a little more firmly on this strand to make it stand a little proud of the G bead.

Make the ninth strand here from 1B, 1F and 1C. Pass the needle through the last A bead of the 15A row at the top of the strand. Pull the thread a little more firmly on this strand to make it stand like a little spike. Pass the needle through the G bead to emerge alongside the first A bead of the next row of 15A around the G bead (fig 9).

Extra Info....
As you continue to add more strands you may find that the thread is getting caught up on the previous fringe strands. Wrap a small plastic bag or scrap of clingfilm around the longer strands already in situ - this will keep them tidy as you continue with the remainder of the strands.

---

7 The next row of 15A is beaded in a similar way with the bead counts adjusted slightly to stagger the effect.

Referring to fig 10 throughout -

Pass the needle through the first 2A of the next row of 15A ready to make the first strand. The needle will be emerging from the second A bead of the 15A.

Make the first strand here from 1A, 1D, 1A, 1D, 1A, 1D, 1A, 1D, 1A, 1E, 1B, 1E, 1B, 1F and 1C. Pass the needle through the second A bead of the 15A row at the top of the strand and the following 2A to emerge from the fourth A bead of the 15A row.

Make the second strand here from 1A, 1D, 1A, 1D, 1A, 1D, 1A, 1E, 1B, 1E, 1B, 1F and 1C. Pass the needle through the fourth A bead of the 15A row at the top of

fig 10

the strand and the following 2A to emerge from the sixth A bead of the 15A row.

Make the third strand here from 1A, 1D, 1A, 1D, 1A, 1E, 1B, 1E, 1B, 1F and 1C. Pass the needle through the sixth A bead of the 15A row at the top of the strand and the following 2A to emerge from the eighth A bead of the 15A row.

Make the fourth strand here from 1A, 1D, 1A, 1E, 1B, 1E, 1B, 1F and 1C. Pass the needle through the eighth A bead of the 15A row at the top of the strand and the following 2A to emerge from the tenth A bead of the 15A row.

Make the fifth strand here from 1A, 1E, 1B, 1E, 1B, 1F and 1C. Pass the needle through the tenth A bead of the 15A row at the top of the strand and the following 2A to emerge from the twelfth A bead of the 15A row.

Make the sixth strand here from 1B, 1E, 1B, 1F and 1C. Pass the needle through the twelfth A bead of the 15A row at the top of the strand and the following 2A to emerge from the fourteenth A bead of the 15A row.

Make the seventh strand here from 2B, 1F and 1C. Pass the needle through the fourteenth A of the 15A row at the top of the strand and the following A bead to emerge from the last A of the 15A row. Pull the thread a little more firmly on this strand to make it stand a little proud of the G bead.

Make the eighth strand here from 1B 1F and 1C. Pass the needle through the last A of the 15A row at the top of the strand. Pull the thread a little more firmly on this strand to make it stand like a little spike. Pass the needle through the G bead to emerge alongside the first A of the next row of 15A around the G bead (fig 10).

Note - you have followed a row of 15A on each occasion. If your row of 15A splits as in fig 4 just follow one side of the split - do not worry about the other 7A - they will be concealed by the overall density of the fringe strands.

8 Repeat steps 4, 5, and 6 and step 7 alternately around the twenty rows of 15A covering the G bead.

When all of the strands are complete, finish off the thread ends neatly and securely. Put the tasselled G bead aside leaving the paper tube in place for the moment.

9 The Slim Tassel - Prepare the needle with 2m of single thread. Approximately 15cm from the end tie the 4mm jump ring onto the thread with a double knot. Thread on 1H and push it up to the jump ring.

Thread on 1A, 1D, 1A, 1D, 1A, 1D, 1A, 1D, 1A, 1D, 1A, 1D, 1A, 1D, 1A, 1D, 1A, 1E, 1B, 1E, 1B, 1F and 1C.

As before, leave aside the last C bead threaded to anchor the strand and pass the needle back up to the top of the strand. Pass the needle through the H bead and through the jump ring at the top (fig 11).

Pass the needle back through the H bead to emerge alongside the top of the strand.

Make the next tassel strand with 3A, 1D, 1A, 1D, 1A, 1D, 1A, 1D, 1A, 1D, 1A, 1D, 1A, 1D, 1A, 1E, 1B, 1E, 1B, 1F and 1C. Pass back up through the H bead, through the jump ring and back down through the H bead ready to make the next tassel strand.

Make the next tassel strand with 1A, 1D, 1A, 1D, 1A, 1D, 1A, 1D, 1A, 1D, 1A, 1D, 1A, 1E, 1B, 1E, 1B, 1F and 1C. Complete the strand as before to bring the needle to emerge from the H bead ready for the next tassel strand.

Make the next tassel strand from 1A, 1D, 1A, 1D, 1A, 1D, 1A, 1D, 1A, 1D, 1A, 1D, 1A, 1E, 1B, 1E, 1B, 1F and 1C. Complete the strand as before. Make two more identical tassel strands.

fig 11

10 To complete the slim tassel you need to make three final tassel strands with the bead sequence 1A, 1D, 1A, 1D, 1A, 1D, 1A, 1D, 1A, 1D, 1A, 1E, 1B, 1E, 1B, 1F and 1C. Finish the final tassel strand with the needle emerging from the top of the H bead alongside the jump ring. Tie the needle end of the thread to the tail end of the thread with a double knot.

Pass the needle through the H bead to neaten and trim closely. Attach the needle to the other thread end and pass through the H bead to neaten before trimming in a similar manner. Dab the threads with a little nail polish or glue where they cross over the jump ring to strengthen the work and prevent them from slipping through the gap in the ring.

11 The Lattice Bead - Repeat step 1 with the second G bead.

Thread on 3C, 1J, 1C, 1A, 1C, 1J, 1C, 1A, 1C, 1J and 3C. Pass the needle through the G bead to bring the new beads into a strap around the side of the G bead (fig 12).

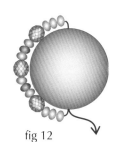

fig 12

12 Following fig 13 thread on 3C, 1J, 1C, 1A and 1C. Pass the needle through the middle J bead of the previous strap and thread on 1C, 1A, 1C, 1J and 3C. Pass the needle through the G bead (fig 13).

Following fig 14 pass the needle through the first 3C and 1J of the previous strap and thread on 1C, 1A, 1C, 1J, 1C, 1A and 1C.

Pass the needle through the last 1J and 3C of the previous strap. Pass the needle through the G bead (fig 14).

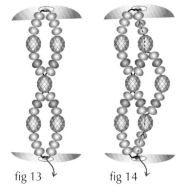

fig 13   fig 14

Repeat step 12 seven more times.
You now need to join the last strap to the first strap.

13 Pass the needle through the first 3C and 1J of the first strap. Thread on 1C, 1A and 1C. Pass the needle through the middle J bead of the last step 12 strap and thread on 1C, 1A and 1C. Pass the needle through the following 1J and 3C of the first strap. Pass the needle through the G bead to complete the beading.

Finish off the thread ends neatly and securely.

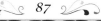

14
Assembling the Tassel - Remove the paper tubes from the 2G beads.

Referring to fig 15 throughout, start by threading the jump ring at the top of the slim tassel onto the middle of the stranded beading wire.

Pass both ends of the wire up through the tasselled G bead. Pull the H bead at the top of the slim tassel up snugly to the hole at the bottom of the G bead - be careful not to snag any of the tassel strands with the wire or the top of the H bead as it nestles into place.

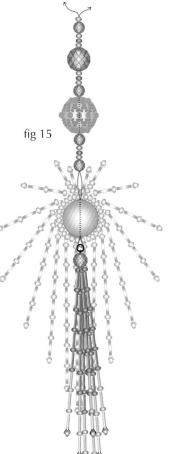

fig 15

With the two wire ends still together thread on 1K, 1C, 1A, 1C and 1K.

Pass the two ends up through the lattice bead. Push all the beads so far down onto the top of the tasselled G bead. The bottom K bead should nestle snugly in the hole at the top of the G bead without jamming any of the short tassel strands there.

With the two wire ends still together thread on 1K, 1C, 1A, 1C, 1L, 1C, 1A, 1C, 1K and 1C. Separate the two wire ends (fig 15).

Make sure that the K beads either side of the lattice G bead are sitting snugly in the holes at either end of the larger bead. Push all of the beads up close to one another.

15
Thread onto each end of the wire 4C, 1B, 3C, 2B, 2C, 3B, 1C, 3B, 1A, 2B, 2A, 1B and 3A. These beads will form the hanging loop. If you want the hanging loop to be longer (or shorter) adjust the bead count now. Add or subtract as many beads as you wish but do it symmetrically so the two sides of the loop match one another.

fig 16

Thread the two French crimps onto one end of the wire. Pass the other end of the wire in the opposite direction through the crimps so the wire ends make an X shape (fig 16). Pull on the wire ends to bring the crimps up snugly to the beads of the hanging loop.

Check everything is sitting properly right along the tassel main stem and the hanging loop. Squash the crimps to secure the wire. If possible pass the wire ends through a few seed beads to either side of the join before trimming to get a neater finish.

Babushka Inspirations
Pine Cone Tassel

This tassel is quite heavy but it feels very luxurious. There are two sizes of metal oval beads (10x5mm & 8x4mm) and 20g of dark cream size 10/0 seed beads setting the cool natural tones. A few larger accent beads above the main G bead finish off the design.

The tasselled G bead is started in the same way but the stranding is a lot shorter than the Babushka design.

The first set of strands (as in steps 4, 5 & 6) starts with 9A, one large oval and 1A. The count reduces by 1A on each subsequent strand.

The second set (as in step 7) starts with 8A, one large oval and 1A and reduces similarly.

A small tapered tassel with strands up to 13A long pulls into the bottom of the G bead to complete the shaping.

The hanging loop is made with a spiral rope technique using the A beads and the smaller ovals.

Thread on 5A and a small oval. Pass through the 5A again.

Thread on 2A and an oval. Pass through the last 3A beads from the previous stitch and the new 2A. Repeat this stitch until the rope is the desired length.

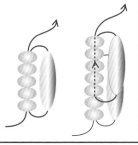

Babushka Inspirations
Midnight Necklace

Certainly a necklace to get noticed - this design uses covered buttons to support the graduated strands so it's comfortable to wear.

You could make an equally stunning pair of earrings by fixing an ear clip onto the back of a decorated button.

You Will Need

Materials

10g of size 10/0 black seed beads A
6g of size 10/0 gunmetal lustre seed beads B
6g of size 10/0 silver lined blue seed beads C
10g of size 3 black twisted bugle beads D
10g of size 3 gunmetal lustre twisted bugle beads E
10g of size 3 transparent blue AB bugle beads F
Forty-five 4mm cobalt blue AB crystal beads G
Six 6mm black crystal beads H
Three 8mm black crystal beads J
Five 22mm covering buttons with removable shanks
Five 35mm squares of stretch velvet-type fabric in black
A reel of black size D beading thread

This Design is Made in Four Stages
The buttons are covered with fabric.
The fringe stranding is added to the buttons.
The completed buttons are stitched together to form the front of the design with the addition of connecting loops for the side straps.
The side straps are added.

16
The Buttons - Remove the shanks from the covering buttons before you start. Depending on the design of the buttons you may be able to slip the shanks out or you may have to cut them away - make sure that you leave no sharp edges.

Use a simple running stitch to gather the first square of velvet fabric ready to go over the button (fig 17). Slip the fabric over the button so the reverse of the fabric shows to the front. Close up the gathers and snap on the backing to give a neat finish.

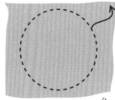

fig 17

Extra Info....
Using a fabric with a pile (like velvet) inside out over the buttons pushes the fabric backing, that you need to stitch through, away from the hard surface of the button. This makes it much easier to make the stitches as you add the decoration.

17
The strands are stitched onto the button in a series of arcs starting with the longest strand of the row at the centre. The strands reduce in length out to either side of each row to taper the design. The following steps will give you a guide to numbers and lengths of strands but you may find that your stitches work out slightly further apart, or closer together, or you may wish to reduce or increase the numbers.

Decorating the Central Button - Prepare the needle with 1.5m of single thread and make a double stitch to secure the thread to the edge of the first button.

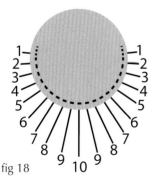

fig 18

Fig 18 shows the position and number of bugle beads in the first row of strands. The nineteen strands attach to the button 1mm in from the edge and spread along approximately two thirds of the circumference.

Position the needle 1mm from the bottom edge and thread on 1A, 1D, 1A, 1D, 1A, 1D, 1A, 1D, 1A, 1D, 1A, 1D, 1A, 1D, 1A, 1E, 1B, 1E, 1B, 1F and 1C (10 bugle beads in total). As fig 6 leave aside the last bead to anchor the strand and pass back up to the button.

Take a small stitch through the fabric to emerge 2.5 to 3mm along ready to make the next tassel strand.

18
The next strand is one bugle bead shorter than the previous strand. Make this new strand with one less repeat of 1A and 1D at the start to make a strand with nine bugle beads (as shown on fig 18).
Repeat to make the third strand 2.5 to 3mm along the path shown in fig 18 making this strand 1A and 1B bead shorter than the previous strand (eight bugle beads in total).
Repeat to make the next seven strands each time removing the top two beads of the previous sequence so the last strand is just 1B, 1F and 1C.

Repeat to make a matching set of strands to the other side of the first long strand (fig 18).

19
Fig 19 shows the positions and lengths for the next row of strands. You can see the strands are a little shorter and the arc is more shallow so the ends of the row can reach the edges of the button at either side.

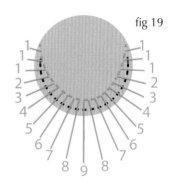

fig 19

The strand sequences are the same as the previous row but start with just nine bugle beads on the first strand. Work as the first row making sure that the last strands come out to the edge of the button.

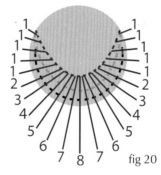

fig 20

20
Fig 20 shows the next row - again the strands are a little shorter and the arc more shallow. Work the row as before.

Work a fourth and fifth row in a similar fashion with a middle strand of six bugles and four bugles respectively as you need to start to reduce the overall strand length a little more.

21
Look at where you are on the button. You need to continue with the rows, reducing as you go, bringing the strand lengths down so that the last row along the top edge contains just 1F bead per stitch.

As the strands shorten towards the top of the button and you remove the last E bead from the sequence do not jump straight to just 1B above the F bead - grade it slightly so you add a few strands with 3B, 1F and 1C beads and 2B, 1F and 1C beads (fig 21).

fig 21

Work to the top edge of the button adding in a few extra stitches 1B, 1F and 1C stitches along the outermost part of the button so it is fully concealed.

To finish you need to go back across the button to add in seven extra strands. These strands need 1G bead added above the F bugle bead. Choose seven different locations and make the correct length strand to match the strands alongside the needle position adding in the extra G bead for a flash of colour and sparkle. Finish off the thread end neatly and securely.

22 Decorating the Medium Buttons - These are made in a similar fashion but with shorter strands.

Start with the longest strand of 1A, 1D, 1A, 1D, 1A, 1E, 1B, 1F and 1C. The next strand on the first row follows the same pattern as the central button with 1A, 1D, 1A, 1E, 1B, 1F and 1C. You will then need to finesse the strand lengths a little more by replacing the top bugle bead with two or three of the appropriate colour of seed bead (as fig 21). This will reduce the sudden step of removing a bugle and each alternate strand is graded more gradually into the next by half a bugle length. Using this more subtle approach work the first four rows of stranding as before.

Stitch 6G into a random cluster directly onto the button in the centre of the remaining space. The margins around the cluster now need to be covered with short strands of 1B, 1F and 1C - if you need to add longer stands to balance out the grading do so. Finish off the thread and make a second button to match.

23 Decorating the Smallest Buttons - Start these with a random cluster of 3H and 6G in the centre of the button. Surround the cluster with short fringe strands of 1B, 1F and 1C. As you work outwards make slightly longer strands to one side of the cluster to keep the overall tapered shape of the previous buttons. Finish off with a few seed bead stitches over and between the crystal beads to bring the whole theme together. Repeat to make a matching button.

24 Making the Connections - Flip the buttons over and arrange so that the longest strands are all pointing downwards and they lie in a pleasing curve. Using a double thread make three 7A links between each pair of button edges.

25 Attach a new double thread to the outer edge of one of the small buttons ready to make the connecting loop for the strap.

Thread on 3A, 1B, 1C, 1J, 1C, 1B, 1G, 1B, 1G, 1B, 1G, 1B, 1G, 1B, 1G, 1B and 1G. Pass the needle through the B bead before the first G bead in the same direction as before (fig 22).

fig 22

Pass the needle through the following G and B beads to complete a circular path finishing with the needle emerging just before the first G bead (as fig 22).

Thread on 1C and pass the needle through the J bead. Thread on 1C, 1B and 3A. Take a stitch through the outer edge of the button 6-8mm from the start (fig 23). Pass the needle through all the beads of this link again to strengthen the work. Finish off this thread and repeat to make an identical ring at the other side of the design.

fig 23

26 The Side Straps - The straps funnel through a simple bugle beaded bead made from F and C beads.

Prepare the needle with 2m of single thread and tie a keeper bead 15cm from the end. Thread on 1C, 1F, 2C, 1F and 1C. Pass the needle through the first 1C, 1F and 1C to bring the bugle beads parallel. Pass the needle through the following 1C, 1F and 1C (fig 24). Thread on 1C, 1F and 1C.

fig 24   fig 25

Pass the needle through the previous 1C, 1F and 1C and the new 1C, 1F and 1C (fig 25). Repeat the stitch in fig 25 four more times to make a ladder 7C beads long.

Roll up the ladder to make a cylinder with 1F at the centre (see fig 26). Secure the cylinder with a few stitches between the columns (fig 26).

end view

fig 26

The thread needs to pass through these holes as you make the strap so do not block them with thread at this stage. Pass the needle through the beads to emerge from one of the outer columns.

27 Thread on 19A. Pass the needle through the G bead ring on the right-hand end of the necklace centre. Pass the needle through the adjacent column on the beaded bead (fig 27).

fig 27

28 Make a mixture of A, B and C beads and thread randomly onto the needle until this side strap is the desired length. Thread on 1G, 1C, 1J, 1C, 1A, 1B and 1A.

Pass the needle back through the last 1C, 1J, 1C and 1G to pull the end three beads into an anchor and create the bead tag end of the clasp (fig 28). Thread on an identical number of mixed A, B and C beads to bring the needle back to the bugle beaded bead.

fig 28

29 Pass the needle through the next column around the bugle beaded bead. Repeat step 27. Make a third strap to match the first two straps passing the needle through the beads of the bead tag and out through the G bead to make a fourth strap.

Repeat to add a third loop of 19A through the G bead ring and a fifth and sixth mixed strap between the bugle beaded bead and the bead tag. Finish off the thread ends neatly and securely.

Repeat to add a similar strap to the other side of the design but this time add a 19A loop to the end to complete the clasp set.

Starstruck Tassel

You Will Need

Materials

12g of size 10/0 silver lined crystal seed beads A
5g of size 2 silver lined crystal bugle beads B
8g of size 3 silver lined crystal bugle beads C
5g of size 8/0 silver lined crystal seed beads D
Fifty-seven 4mm crystal AB fire polished faceted beads E
Ten 12x6mm crystal AB cross-hole drop beads F
Ten 6mm crystal AB fire polished faceted beads G
A reel of white size D beading thread

Tools

A size 13 beading needle
A pair of scissors to trim the threads

*The finished length of this tassel is 29.5cm
including the hanging loop.*

Mathematicians might call this tassel an embellished stellated icosahedron! The star is straightforward to build, but it does take patience to get the tension correct, so this project is graded as a little more difficult than some. It's extremely sparkly & makes a fantastic Christmas decoration.

The Tassel is Made in Five Stages

An icosahedron for the centre of the star.
Star points are added to each of the icosahedron faces.
The star pendants for the bottom of the tassel strands.
The tassel strands.
The hanging loop.

1 The Icosahedron - This is a twenty-sided regular polygon made with interlinked triangles. The triangles are built from the B bead bugles with an A seed bead at each corner. It isn't difficult to build but you need to manage your tension throughout - pull the thread quite firmly as you complete each triangle so the beads all pull up snugly against one another.

> ### Extra Info....
> You may find that conditioning the thread with a little beeswax before you start will help it to run through the beads a little better and help you to maintain the firm tension in the thread more easily.

Prepare the needle with 1.5m of double thread and tie a keeper bead 15cm from the end.

Thread on 1B, 1A, 1B, 1A, 1B and 1A. Pass the needle through the first 1B, 1A and 1B beads to create the first triangle (fig 1).

fig 1   fig 2

2 Thread on 1A, 1B, 1A, 1B and 1A. Pass the needle through the B bead on the previous triangle and the first 1A and 1B of the new triangle (fig 2).

Note - the triangles are joined together through the B bead only - the A beads play no part in the links.

3 Thread on 1A, 1B, 1A, 1B and 1A. Pass the needle through the B bead on the previous triangle and the following 1A and 1B of the new triangle (fig 3).

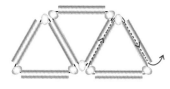

fig 3

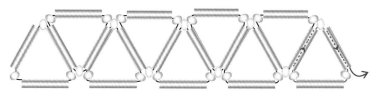

fig 4

Repeat steps 2 and 3 three more times to make a straight chain of nine triangles (fig 4).

4 You need to create a tenth triangle to link the first triangle to the ninth triangle.

Referring to fig 5, thread on 1A. Pass the needle through the first B bead of the first triangle and thread on 1A, 1B and 1A. Pass the needle down the last B bead of the ninth triangle (see fig 5).

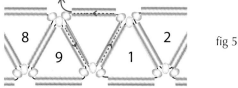

8   2   fig 5
9   1

Pass the needle through the first A bead just added, the first B of the first triangle and the following 1A and 1B (fig 5).

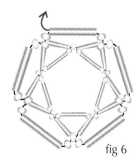

fig 6

You will now have a little drum of A and B beads with the needle emerging from a B bead on the top edge of the drum.

Fig 6 shows a top view of the drum - the next stage is to add five inter-linked triangles that will form a pointed cap on the end of the drum.

The following diagrams will show just the top row of the drum. The added cap beads will be shown in pink to help you to differentiate these beads from those of the drum. Pay particular attention to the direction of each stitch as shown in the figs.

5 Thread on 1A, 1B, 1A, 1B and 1A. Pass the needle through the B bead on the top edge of the drum and the following 1A and 1B just added (fig 7).

fig 7

6 Thread on 1A, 1B and 1A.

Referring to fig 8 pass the needle through the next B bead around the top of the drum and thread on 1A. Pass the needle through the adjacent B bead of the previous triangle and the first 1A and 1B of the new triangle (fig 8).

fig 8

fig 9

Thread on 1A and pass through the next 1B bead around the top row of the drum (see fig 9).

Thread on 1A, 1B and 1A.

Pass the needle through the adjacent B bead of the previous triangle to pull up the new triangle.

Pass through the following 1A of this new triangle, the B bead from the top row of the drum again and the following 1A and 1B of the new triangle (fig 9).

7 Thread on 1A, 1B and 1A.

Referring to fig 10 pass the needle through the next B bead around the top of the drum and thread on 1A.
Pass the needle through the adjacent B bead of the previous triangle and the first 1A and 1B just added (fig 10).

fig 10

8 To complete the cap on this end of the drum you need to link the triangle made in step 5 to the last triangle made.

fig 11

Referring to fig 11 thread on 1A and pass through the next B bead around the top of the drum.

Thread on 1A and pass through the adjacent B bead of the first triangle.

Thread on 1A and pass the needle through the following B bead of the previous triangle (fig 11).

This completes the five-triangle cap to this end of the drum. You now need to make an identical cap at the other end of the drum.

Note - If you run short of thread do not tie off the thread ends as you will obstruct the holes in the beads. Cut the needle from the thread, leaving the tails as long as possible, so you can return to them later to fasten off securely.

Start a new thread with a keeper bead 15cm from the end. Pass the needle through the work to continue the beading without using any knots. These ends can also be secured later.

9 Reposition the needle through the beads of the work, to emerge from one of the B beads at the other end of the drum as in fig 6 ready to make the cap at this end.

Repeat steps 5 to 8 inclusive to make a five-triangle cap at this end of the drum.

You have completed the icosahedron.

10 At this stage the beadwork will feel a little soft and it will deform quite easily, but as you add the star points, it will become more firm.

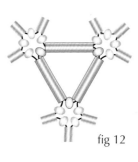

fig 12

Take a close look at the beadwork before you start the star points.

Each three-sided star point will be supported by the 3B beads of each triangle.

At each corner junction there are 5A beads corresponding to the five triangles that meet at that position (see fig 12). The five triangles form a pentagon around the 5A beads at the centre.

As you work across the icosahedron, adding the points in the next few steps, you will need to pass the needle through each set of 5A beads to pull them up into a tight ring. This will stiffen the shape considerably.

11 The Star Points - Each point is made from three C beads topped off by an E bead and a picot of A beads.

Each C bead straddles across the A bead at one corner of the triangular base. The thread path passes from the bottom of the C bead to both of the B beads to either side of the A bead at the corner making the point very stable. The C beads are shown in lilac in the following diagrams.

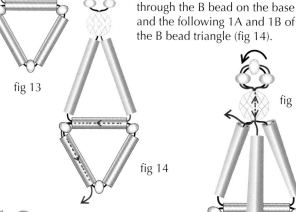

The needle will be emerging from a B bead. This B bead will be the first side of the triangle to support the star point.

Thread on 1C, 1E and 3A. Pass the needle back down the E bead to pull the 3A into a picot (fig 13).

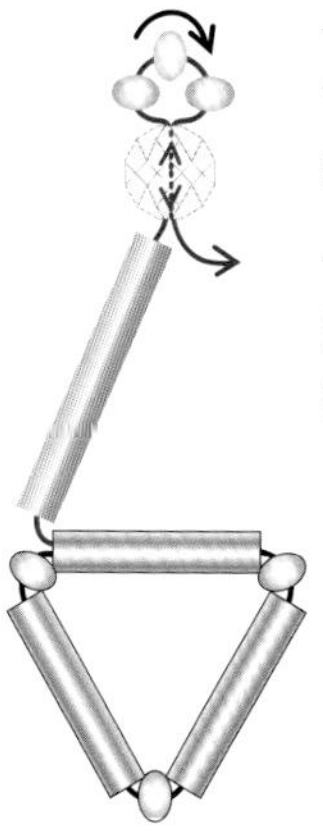

Thread on 1C. Pass the needle through the B bead on the base and the following 1A and 1B of the B bead triangle (fig 14).

fig 13

fig 14

12 Thread on 1C. Pass the needle up through the E bead and the 3A beads of the picot added in fig 13. Pass the needle back down the E bead (fig 15).

Pass the needle down through the first C bead of the star point and the second B bead of the base triangle (see fig 16). Pass through the following 1A and 1B of the base triangle (fig 16).

Note - the needle did not pass through the A bead at the bottom of the C bead when passing down from the E bead. The C beads connect directly to the B beads of the base triangle.

13 To complete the point, the B bead on the third side of the base triangle has to be connected to the adjacent C beads of the point.

Examine the beadwork and identify the B bead on the base triangle that the point is not yet connected to (the needle is emerging from one end of this B bead).

Pass the needle up through the closest C bead of the point and down through the C bead at the other end of the same B bead. Pass through the B bead to bring the point to sit centrally above the base triangle (fig 17).

fig 15

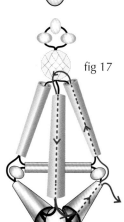

fig 16

fig 17

14 The needle is emerging from the third B bead of the base triangle that supports the point just completed. This B bead now becomes the first B bead of the new base triangle for the next star point. Work this star point following steps 11, 12 and 13 as before.

You now need a plan to move forward across the surface of the icosahedron. As described in step 10 the base triangles form sets of five around the 5A groupings on the icosahedron. The most systematic way to make the points is to work the five base triangles around one group of 5A before moving onto the next group of 5A.

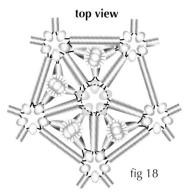

top view

fig 18

15 Make the next two points surrounding the group of 5A (fig 18).

Before you make the fifth point pass the needle through the 5A bead group at the centre whilst you can still gain reasonable access to these beads. This will help to stiffen the work (fig 18). Make the fifth point to complete a set of five points around one group of 5A.

If you look at the work you have the first two points already made of each of the next five 5A groups. Choose one of these new groups of 5A and repeat step 15.

Repeat until you have completed all twenty points, remembering to strengthen each group of 5A before you close it off completely.

Leave the thread ends unfinished as you still need to pass the needle through some of the beads to add the tassel strands and the hanging loop.

16 The Star Pendants - Prepare the needle with 1.2m of single thread and tie a keeper bead 15cm from the end. Thread on 1A, 1D, 1A, 1D, 1A, 1D, 1A, 1D, 1A and 1D. Pass the needle through the first A bead to bring the beads into a circle (fig 19).

Pass the needle through the beads once more to make the circle a little more firm. Finish with the needle emerging from the first 1A as fig 19.

fig 19

fig 20

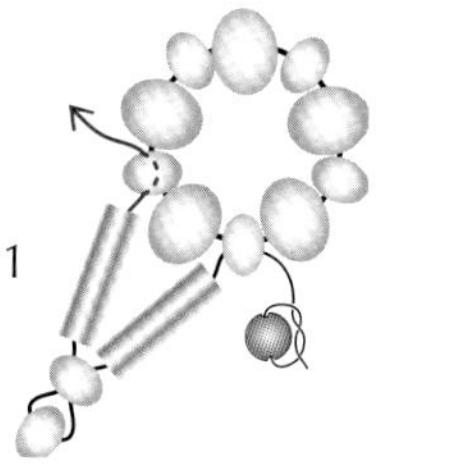

fig 21

17 Thread on 1B and 2A. Pass the needle back through the first A bead of the 2A just added to bring the last A bead up into an anchor (fig 20).

Thread on 1B. Pass the needle through the next A bead around the circle to form the first point on the star (fig 21).

18
Repeat step 17 four more times to add a further four points to the star (fig 22).

The needle will be emerging from the bottom A bead as fig 22.

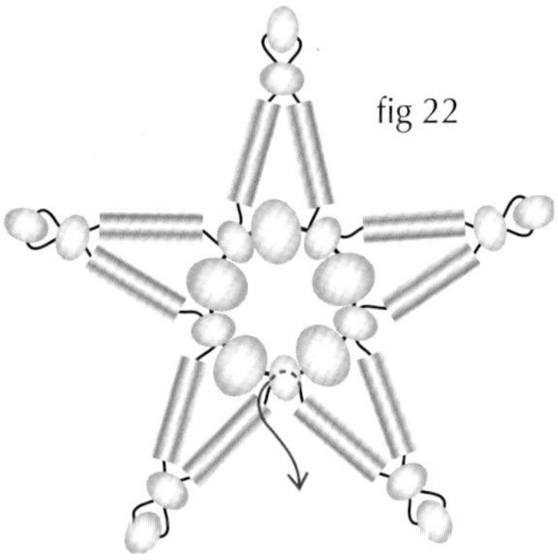

fig 22

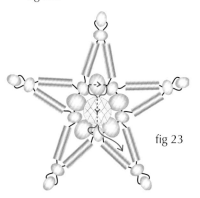

fig 23

19
Thread on 1E. Pass the needle through the D bead on the opposite side of the ring to the bottom A bead.

Pass back through the E bead to pull it into the centre of the ring (fig 23). Pass the needle through the bottom A bead in the same direction as before to centralise the stitch across the centre of the ring.

The E bead will be sitting proud in the centre of the ring.

Flip the star over passing the needle between the beads to come through to this side of the work - it should still be emerging from the bottom A bead of the ring as before.

Repeat Step 19 to add an E bead to this side of the ring.

To make the points of the star a little more firm pass the needle through the five points of the star in turn, following the same thread path as in fig 21, to emerge through the A bead at the bottom of the star as in fig 22.

fig 24

20
Thread on 3A, 1D, 5A, 1F and 4A.

Pass the needle up through the first 1A of the 5A sequence and the following 1D and 3A (fig 24).

Pass the needle through the A bead at the bottom of the star in the same direction as before to centralise the drop below the star.

Finish off the thread ends neatly and securely. Set the pendant aside for the moment.

Make two more of these star pendants to match.

Extra Info....
When you have made the first four tassel strands tie them together loosely with a scrap of thread - it makes it easier to locate the position of the next six strands.

21
The Tassel Strands - Each tassel strand is made with a single thread which runs from the tip of the picot on one of the star points, down to the bottom of the strand and back up to the point of the picot. The holes in the B beads of the tassel top are already very full of thread so it may not be possible to reposition the needle through these beads to be in the correct position for the next tassel strand. You may have to start and finish a new thread for some, if not all, of the strands.

Do not force the needle through the A and B beads of the icosahedron as you may break a bead which would spoil the work - find another path for the needle or finish the thread and start a new thread for the next strand.

22
Pick a point on the tassel top star and look directly down onto the point. This point will be connected through the base triangle to three more points. The central point will support the longest fringe strand and the three points surrounding it will carry the next three longest strands.

Prepare the needle with 1.2m of single thread and tie a keeper bead 15cm from the end.

Pass the needle through the E bead of the chosen point and the following 2A to emerge through the tip of the picot (fig 25).

fig 25

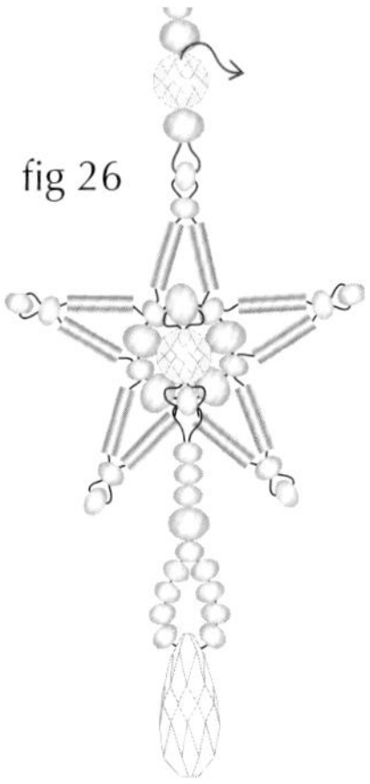

fig 26

23
Thread on 40A, 1C, 1A, 1C, 1A, 1C, 1A, 1C, 1A, 1D, 1E, 1D, 3A, 1D, 1G, 1D, 2A, 1D, 1E and 1D.

Pick up the first prepared star pendant. Pass the needle through the A bead at the tip of the point immediately opposite the F bead dangle and back up through the last 1D and 1E of the strand (fig 26).

24
Pass the needle back up the remaining beads of the strand to emerge 1A before the top.

Thread on 1A and pass the needle through the A bead on the tip of the picot in the same direction as before to centre the strand beneath this A bead (fig 27).

This completes the first tassel strand.

Locate one of the three points surrounding this central point. If possible, reposition the needle through the beads of the current point and the base triangle to emerge through the A bead tip of the newly selected point, ready to make the next strand.

If this is not possible, finish off the two thread ends for the current point neatly and securely. Start a new thread as in step 22 to emerge through the A bead tip of the selected point for the next strand.

fig 27

25 Thread on 33A, 1C, 1A, 1C, 1A, 1C, 1A, 1C, 1A, 1D, 1E, 1D, 3A, 1D, 1G, 1D, 2A, 1D, 1E, 1A, 1D, 5A, 1F and 4A.

fig 28

Pass the needle back up through the first A bead of the 5A just threaded and the following 1B to form a loop to support the F bead (fig 28).

Pass the needle up through the beads of the strand as before to emerge 1A before the top. Thread on 1A and centralise the strand below the picot tip as in fig 27.

You have two points remaining around the central point supporting the longest tassel strand. Reposition the needle to emerge through the A bead tip on the next point to be worked or, as before, start a new thread to emerge through the A bead tip ready to make the next strand.

For the new strand thread on 22A, 1C, 1A, 1C, 1A, 1C, 1A, 1C, 1A, 1D, 1E, 1D, 3A, 1D, 1G, 1D, 2A, 1D, 1E, 1A, 1D, 5A, 1F and 4A. Make the end of the strand as in fig 28 and complete the strand as before.

Reposition the needle for the third point around the central strand as before.

For this strand thread on 17A, 1C, 1A, 1C, 1A, 1C, 1A, 1C, 1A, 1D, 1E, 1D, 3A, 1D, 1G, 1D, 2A, 1D, 1E, 1A, 1D, 5A, 1F and 4A. Make the end of the strand as in fig 28 and complete the strand as before.

26 Look again at the 20-pointed star - you now have four tassel strands attached to the central point and the three points surrounding it. There are six points connected through the base triangles to the three points just worked. These six points will support the a tassel strand each.

You have two star pendants and four F beads remaining - one for each of the six strands. You need to work around the six points in turn to add the final strands. Choose one point to start on and either reposition the needle or attach a new thread to emerge through this picot tip.

27 Thread on 21A, 1C, 1A, 1C, 1A, 1C, 1A, 1C, 1A, 1D, 1E, 1D, 3A, 1D, 1G, 1D, 2A, 1D, 1E and 1D. Add a star pendant to the bottom of the strand as in fig 26 and complete the strand as before. Move onto the second point of the six.

For the second strand thread on 2A, 1C, 1A, 1C, 1A, 1C, 1A, 1C, 1A, 1D, 1E, 1D, 3A, 1D, 1G, 1D, 2A, 1D, 1E, 1A, 1D, 5A, 1F and 4A. Make the bottom of the strand as in fig 28 and complete the strand as before. Move onto the third point of the six.

For the third strand thread on 2A, 1C, 1A, 1D, 1E, 1D, 3A, 1D, 1G, 1D, 2A, 1D, 1E, 1A, 1D, 5A, 1F and 4A Make the bottom of the strand as in fig 28 and complete the strand as before. Move onto the fourth point of the six.

For the fourth strand thread on 9A, 1C, 1A, 1C, 1A, 1C, 1A, 1C, 1A, 1D, 1E, 1D, 3A, 1D, 1G, 1D, 2A, 1D, 1E and 1D. Add a star pendant to the bottom of the strand as in fig 26 and complete the strand as before. Move onto the fifth point of the six.

28 For the fifth strand thread on 2A, 1C, 1A, 1C, 1A, 1D, 1E, 1D, 3A, 1D, 1G, 1D, 2A, 1D, 1E, 1A, 1D, 5A, 1F and 4A. Make the bottom of the strand as in fig 28 and complete the strand as before. Move onto the last point of the six.

For the last strand thread on 3A, 1D, 1E, 1D, 3A, 1D, 1G, 1D, 2A, 1D, 1E, 1A, 1D, 5A, 1F and 4A. Make the bottom of the strand as in fig 28 and complete the strand as before.

Finish off all of the remaining thread ends neatly and securely.

29 The Hanging Loop - Make a star motif as in steps 16 to 19 inclusive. The needle will be emerging from the bottom A bead of the ring as in fig 22.

Thread on 3A, 1C and 3A. Pick up the 20-pointed star and locate the point immediately opposite the longest tassel strand. Pass the needle through the A bead at the tip of this point. Pass the needle back up through the beads just added and through the A bead at the bottom of the small star motif in the same direction as before.
Pass the needle down and up the A and C beads just added to strengthen the connection to the 20-pointed star.

Pass the needle through the beads of the small star motif to emerge from the top A bead on the opposite point (fig 29).

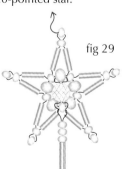

fig 29

Thread on 5A, 1D, 1A, 1B, 1A and 1D followed by nine repeats of 1A, 1D, 1A and 1E. Then thread on 1A, 1D and 1A.

Pass the needle down through the 1D and 1A immediately above the B bead, the B bead itself and the remaining beads back down to the top of the small star.
Pass the needle through the A bead at the tip of the small star point. Pass the needle through all of the beads just added two more times to strengthen the loop and finish off the thread end neatly and securely.

Starstruck Inspirations *Gothika Tassel*

A tassel of two stars - one with twenty points just like the Starstruck Tassel design and a new one with eight points. To balance out the proportions the tassel strands are made much shorter to allow for a longer strand above the larger star.

You Will Need

Materials

6g of size 10/0 black seed beads A
5g of size 2 black bugle beads B
8g of size 3 silver lined red bugle beads C
5g of size 10/0 silver lined red seed beads D
Twenty-eight 4mm black fire polished faceted beads E
Ten 8x6mm red crystal rondelles F
Eleven 6x4mm black crystal rondelles G
One 8mm black crystal bead H
One 6mm red crystal bead J
A reel of black size D beading thread

Tools

A size 13 beading needle
A pair of scissors to trim the threads

The Tassel is Made in Six Stages
An icosahedron for the centre of the large star.
Star points are added to each of the icosahedron faces.
The octahedron for the middle of the smaller star.
The points for the smaller star.
The tassel strands.
The hanging loop.

Make an icosahedron as in steps 1 to 9 inclusive.

Make the twenty points of the star as in steps 10 to 15 inclusive substituting the A beads for D beads to give the star points a red tip.

30 The Octahedron
- Repeat steps 1, 2 and 3 to make a chain of five triangles only (fig 30).

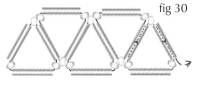

fig 30

fig 31

You need to create a sixth triangle to link the first triangle to the fifth triangle.

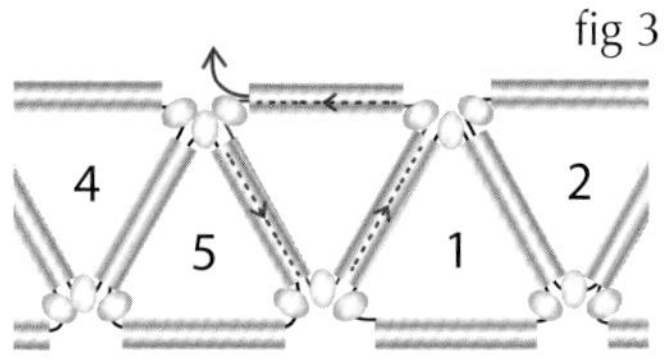

Following fig 31 throughout, thread on 1A. Pass the needle through the first B bead of the first triangle and thread on 1A, 1B and 1A. Pass the needle down the last B bead of the fifth triangle.

Pass the needle through the first A bead just added, the first B bead of the first triangle and the following 1A and 1B (fig 31).

The finished length of this tassel is 19cm not including the hanging loop.

31 Once again you have created a little drum of A and B beads with the needle emerging from a B bead on the top edge of the drum (fig 32).

fig 32

There are three B beads around the end of the drum. You need to link these 3B together with 1A as a spacer between each pair.

fig 33

Thread on 1A. Pass the needle through the next 1B around the top of the drum.

Repeat twice (fig 33).

This will make this end of the drum much more stable.

Pass the needle through to the other end of the drum and repeat. If you count the faces of the shape now you will find that you have the eight triangles of the octahedron, as required, with 4A beads in a group at each intersection.

32 Following steps 11, 12 and 13 make the first star point with D beads instead of A beads to give the point a red tip as before.

Repeat to add a point to each of the remaining seven faces of the octahedron - make sure you remember to pass the needle through the 4A beads at the intersections of the triangles just as for the 5A beads on the icosahedron made before.

Leave the thread ends unfinished.

33 The Tassel Strands - There are ten tassel strands to dangle from the large star as on the Starstruck design. Read through steps 21 and 22 and start a new 1.2m thread as in fig 25.

Thread on 1D, 4A, 1B, 1A, 1B, 1A, 1D, 1A, 1F, 1A, 1D, 1G, 1D and 3A.
Leaving aside the last 3A beads to anchor the strand, pass the needle back up through the last D bead threaded (fig 34) and the following beads to emerge at the tip of the star point.

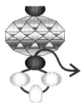

fig 34

fig 35

Pass the needle through the D bead at the tip of the star in the same direction as before (fig 35).

Locate one of the three star points surrounding this central point.

If possible reposition the needle through the beads of the current point and the base triangle to emerge through the tip A bead of the newly selected point ready to make the next strand. If this is not possible finish off the two thread ends for the current point neatly and securely. Start a new thread as in fig 25 to emerge through the tip A bead of the selected point for the next strand.

34 Thread on 1D, 3A, 1B, 1A, 1D, 1A, 1F, 1A, 1D, 1G, 1D and 3A. Leaving aside the last 3A to anchor the bottom of the strand, complete the strand as before. Make an identical strand from the other two points surrounding the central strand repositioning the needle or using a new thread as necessary.

The six surrounding points need a similar strand. Following the same technique make a strand from each of these points from 1D, 2A, 1D, 1A, 1F, 1A, 1D, 1G, 1D and 3A.

Finish off all of the thread ends attached to the large star.

35 Attach a needle to the longest thread still joined to the small star and pass it through to emerge from the tip of one of the points. Thread on 1D, 1A, 1B, 1A, 1B, 1A, 1B, 1A, 1B, 1A, 1B, 1A, 1J, 1A, 1D, 1H, 1D, 1A, 1B, 1A and 1D. Pass the needle through the tip of the large star immediately opposite the longest tassel strand to link the two stars together. Pass the needle back up through the beads just added to emerge 1D before the top of the strand. Thread on 1D and pass the needle through the D bead at the tip of the star point in the same direction as before (as fig 27).

Pass the needle down and up through the strand just added one more time to strengthen before finishing off this thread end neatly and securely.

36 The Hanging Loop - If necessary attach a new 70cm thread to emerge through the top point of the small star (immediately opposite the connection to the large star just made). Thread on 1D, 1A, 1D, 1G, 1D and 50A.

Pass the needle back through the last D bead to pull up the loop and the following beads just added to emerge at the top of the star point. Pass the needle through the D bead at the tip of the point and back up through all the beads of the loop to strengthen it.

Finish off this thread end and all of the remaining thread ends neatly and securely.

Seasons Tassel

Spring

Summer

The finished length of this tassel is 40cm including the hanging loop. It measures 29cm below the hanging loop

The finished length of this tassel is 44cm including the hanging loop. It measures 28cm below the hanging loop.

Winter

The finished length
of this tassel is
26cm including the
crystal donut.
It hangs on a cord
rather than a
beaded loop.

Autumn

The finished length
of this tassel is
28cm including the
hanging loop.
It measures 23cm
below the hanging
loop.

The Seasons Tassel is designed to let your imagination go wild. The first new shoots of Spring; Summer seaside days; the falling leaves of Autumn and the first snow of Winter silhouetted against a midnight sky. This is a technique that anyone with a passion for beads or embroidery will enjoy.

These designs are all built around a plain wooden bead. In contrast to the Babushka, Balmoral and Windsor Tassels, where the large base bead is covered with a regular pattern of beadwork, here the beads are embroidered over the surface to form a variety of patterns and textures.

All four of the Seasons designs start by covering the base bead with a stitchable surface.

Seasons Tassel
Covering the Base Bead

You Will Need
these items in the appropriate colours for
your chosen project

Materials

One 30mm round wooden base bead
50cm of 15mm wide knitted tubular wire
A reel of thread

Tools

A size 10 beading needle
A pair of general-purpose scissors to cut the wire tubing
A pair of scissors to trim the threads
A knitting needle or similar that will fit through the hole
in the wooden bead (see below)

The knitting needle (or a smooth pencil or dowel) has to fit easily through the hole in the wooden bead but not be too loose as it needs to stay in place as you work.

1 Examine the large wooden bead - you may be able to see small wooden fibres pushing into the hole and around the edges of the hole - it is important that the hole is smooth. Push the knitting needle through the hole to smooth the fibres.

Cut 25cm of knitted tubular wire. Twist the last 2cm of the tubing into a point and pass it through the wooden bead so the bead sits halfway along the length. Cut off the twisted end of the tube as it will be too distorted to work with any further. Push the knitting needle down the central hole of the tubing and through the hole in the bead so the bead sits centrally on the knitting needle.

Extra Info....

If you are changing the colour scheme of the design choose a knitted tube colour that complements the darkest shade of beads in your palette. If you choose a paler shade the wire covering will tend to be more noticeable between the beads of the decoration.

2 Open out the first end of the tube and stretch it backwards over the outside of the bead to cover the surface (fig 1).

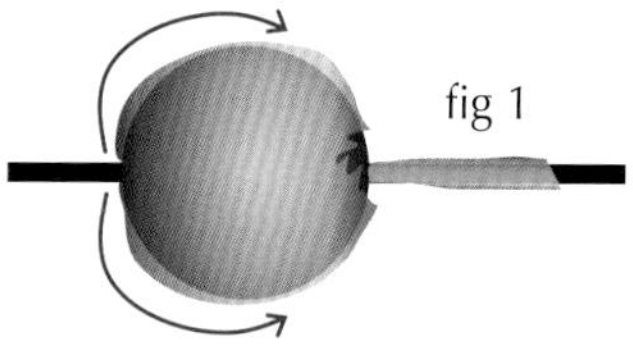

fig 1

Repeat with the other end of the tube to make a double layer of mesh over the surface (fig 2).

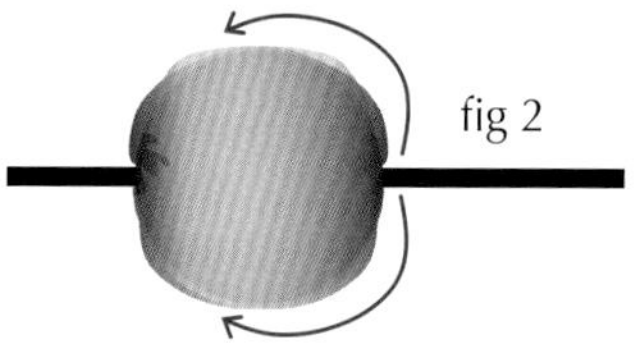

fig 2

Trim away the excess tubing and tuck the cut edge under (not down the hole). Squeeze the bead all over to make the mesh fit the base bead closely.

3 Cut a second length of wire tubing and repeat steps 1 and 2 to give you four layers of mesh in total over the surface of the wooden bead.

The mesh needs to be secured with a thread binding before you can apply the beads.

4 Prepare the beading needle with 2m of single thread. Make a double stitch into the mesh on the surface of the bead to start the thread.

fig 3

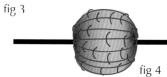

fig 4

Pass the needle through the wooden bead sliding it along the surface of the knitting needle.

Pass the needle through the wooden bead again to bring the thread into a strap over the surface of the mesh (fig 3).

Repeat all the way around the circumference of the wooden bead to make 15-20 straps of thread holding the mesh close to the bead.

To stop the layers of mesh from moving across one another make 20-25 stitches at 90° to the straps over the surface of the mesh: make the stitches 8-10mm long and through all of the layers of mesh (fig 4). Finish off the thread end with a double stitch into the mesh.

Keep the knitting needle in place for the remainder of the decoration of the base bead to maintain the integrity of the hole.

The Surface Can Now be Decorated in Many Ways

It can be covered with small seed beads, or you can introduce feature beads or pre-prepare other motifs to apply to the surface.

You can apply other 'found objects' - buttons, old earrings or a brooch, sequins, scraps of lace or shells - whatever you find inspiring or that matches your scheme.

Different types of thread, a variety of gauges of knitted and plain wire, fancy yarn or ribbon can be stitched through the mesh or couched onto the mesh.

Traditional embroidery stitches can be used to add a smooth glossy finish or piled randomly between clusters of beads to create a jumble of texture and tone.

Planning Your Design

As the surface is curved it is difficult to make a regular repeating pattern with these techniques. You can divide the surface into defined sections with temporary stitches in a contrasting thread but it is best to be a little more flexible in your approach.

Bring all of your materials together and decide whether you want the decoration to be quite simple over the base bead and to concentrate the pattern within the tassel strands - like the Winter Tassel project, or to make the large bead the eyectaching feature - like the Autumn Tassel project. For a softer effect the colours are graded through the Summer Tassel project with the decoration more densely applied to the large bead and the bottom of the strands whereas the Spring Tassel project has a more elaborate hanging loop and a heavily decorated top bead.

Getting Started

The surface of the base bead can look very large and dauntingly plain before you begin the decoration. Starting off is often the most difficult part of the design. You need to break the surface down into smaller regions before you start to think about details.

In the Summer Tassel project, several continuous waves of seed beads are stitched around the base bead dividing the surface into smaller, more manageable sections. These smaller sections suit the scale of the beads better and each pocket can then be worked on individually. Similarly the Button Tassel (right) has undulating rows of textured yarn couched onto the surface with a finer, multi-coloured woollen thread. The gaps are filled with smaller woollen stitches and the buttons applied with an embroidery cotton on top.

The Autumn Tassel divides the surface into radiating zones. Pick a spot and apply a large feature bead (in this case a beaded leaf). Space the remaining large feature beads across the surface and then work outwards from them. The Winter Tassel works in a similar way with radiating stitches of embroidery cotton that expand until they touch one another.

The Spring Tassel starts at the top and adds beads in a series of concentric circles. The circles are not all equal in width as a variety of shapes and sizes of beads are used to add texture and interest, so some circles wiggle up and down quite a lot. Towards the bottom the circles turn into higgledy-piggledy vertical stitches to resemble plant stems.

The Tassel Stranding

As in the Windsor, Balmoral, Persian and Turkish Tassel designs the tassel strands are made separately and pulled up to the bottom of the decorated base bead on a length of stranded beading wire. See also the basic tassel instructions on page 12.

The strands can be -
Random lengths as in the Spring Tassel
Graded colours and lengths like the Summer Tassel.
Graded strand lengths with a variety of weight beads at the bottom similar to the Autumn Tassel.
Identical weighted ends on graded strand lengths as in the Winter Tassel.

The Hanging Loop

You should use the beads of the hanging loop above the base bead to balance out the design proportions.

The Spring Tassel uses a loose plait to add width and keep with the naturalistic theme.
The Summer Tassel adds a smaller beaded bead and a graded selection of beads on the loop to match the tassel.
The Autumn Tassel adds a textured link, a small beaded bead and a repeat pattern on the loop itself.
The Winter Tassel uses a ring to link to a silky cord loop picking up the embroidered texture on the decorated bead.

You Will Need

Materials

25g of size 10/0 chalk pea green seed beads A

20g of additional contrasting seed beads in sizes 10/0, 8/0 & 6/0 in oranges, teals and gold B

Approximately two hundred and fifty 6mm to 10mm feature beads to include fifty top-holed leaves & drops, ninety through-hole flower shapes, and an assortment of crystal & gold metallic beads in similar colours C

Two 8x6mm pale green crystal rondelles D
One 30mm round wooden base bead
50cm of 15mm wide leaf green knitted tubular wire
80cm of a fine gauge premium stranded beading wire
Two gold French crimps
A reel of ash size D beading thread

Tools

A size 10 beading needle
A pair of scissors to trim the threads
A pair of flat-faced pliers or similar to secure the crimps

The Tassel is made in Five Stages

The base bead is covered in knitted wire.
The surface of the base bead is decorated.
The tassel stranding.
The hanging loop.
The small branched tassel strands at the bottom of the decorated bead are added to complete the project.

Referring to steps 1 to 4 on page 102, cover the 30mm base bead with the tubular wire ready to begin the decoration.

Put aside 40 flower beads for the hanging loop.

5 Decorating the Base Bead -
The decoration starts close to the top hole and works down the base bead in a series of concentric circles.
Prepare the needle with 1.5m of double thread and make a double stitch into the mesh 3-4mm from the top hole of the bead to anchor the thread.

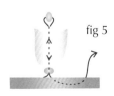

fig 5

Thread on 1A, a flower bead and 1B. Pass the needle back through the flower bead and the A bead. Make a small stitch through the mesh to draw the flower upright (fig 5).

Make a small stitch through the mesh to emerge 4mm from the first flower and repeat (fig 6).

Repeat until you have a circle of flower beads around the hole.

fig 6

6 Working down over the base bead repeat to make a second circle quite close to the first circle adding in two or three leaves to add more texture (fig 7).

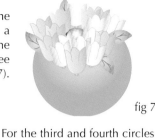

fig 7

fig 8

For the third and fourth circles space the flowers and leaves out a little further adding in a few short stitches of three or four A & B beads in the gaps (fig 8).

Continue down the mesh making further circles, fading out the larger leaves and flowers, but adding more seed bead stitches and a few smaller feature beads.

Make the seed bead stitches a little longer as you reach the middle of the base bead, bringing some stitches right down to the hole at the bottom so they resemble stems for the flowers around the top of the mesh. Work until the mesh is completely covered. Finish off the thread neatly and securely.

7 The Tassel Stranding - The straight tassel strands are worked mainly in A beads. Short sequences of 3B beads are added at intervals and 3-4C beads are blended into the length towards the bottom.

Prepare the needle with 2m of single thread and tie a size 6/0 B bead 15cm from the end. Pass the needle through 1D ready to begin the first tassel strand.

Referring to the basic tassel instructions on page 12 begin to thread on the beads for the first tassel strand.

Start with 5cm of A beads adding in four or five sets of 3B in the first 10-12cm. Now add a C bead with 1B on either side. Add two more C beads at 1-2cm intervals bringing the strand to 16-18cm in total.

Pass the needle back up through the strand beads, through the D bead and the size 6/0 B bead right at the top. Pass down the D bead ready to make the next strand.

Repeat to complete 13-15 tassel strands in various, slightly shorter lengths.

Finish off the thread ends neatly and securely.

8 The Hanging Loop - Cut the stranded beading wire in half and thread both lengths through the D bead at the top of the tassel strands. Remove the knitting needle from the decorated bead and pass all four wire ends up through this bead and 1D. Pull firmly on the wire ends so the D beads fit snugly into the holes at either end of the decorated bead.

You have 40 reserved flower beads - allocate five of these flower beads to each wire thread end. Thread 1A and one flower bead (pointing upwards) onto each end.

Picking up the relative colour densities in the tassel strands, thread sufficient A, B and a few of the smaller C beads onto the first wire thread end to space out the remaining four flowers into a 14cm fully-beaded length. Repeat with the other three ends.

The wire thread ends need to be joined together in pairs to make two complete hanging loops of exactly the same length. Thread one crimp onto the first wire end. Pass the end of the second wire in the opposite direction through the crimp. Pass both ends through a few beads to either side of the crimp (fig 9).

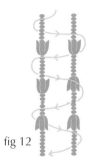

fig 9

Repeat with the third and fourth of wire ends. Check the loops are the same length as one another and squash the crimps to secure the work. Trim the excess wire away.

9 Prepare the needle with 1.5m of double thread and tie a keeper bead 15cm from the end. You will need the remaining 20 flower beads saved for the hanging loop.

Following the same bead sequences you have already used on the hanging loop thread on 2cm of A and B beads. Thread on one flower bead and 2B.

Pass the needle back through the first B bead of the 2B just added and the flower bead. Pass the needle through the last bead on the main strand in the same direction as before (fig 10).

fig 10

Repeat to add a further 2cm of A and B seed beads and a second flower. Repeat until you have used all of the remaining reserved flowers - finish with 2cm of A and B beads. The strap will be approximately 42cm in length.

10 Pass the needle through one of the upturned flower beads that you added at the very start of the loops in step 8 to emerge at the surface of the base bead (see fig 11). Fasten off the thread here on the mesh with a double stitch (fig 11). Neaten and trim the thread end.

fig 11

You now have two completed loops and one strung length attached to the top of the beaded bead.

Following fig 12 hold the two complete hanging loops parallel to one another and 1cm apart. Weave the strung length backwards and forwards between these loops, to form a loose plait effect, bringing the keeper bead around to the top of the decorated bead at the other end of the loops. Remove the keeper bead and attach the needle to these ends.

fig 12

Pass the needle through one of the upturned flowers associated with this end of the loops (see fig 11) and fasten off the end as before.

11 The Branched Fringes -

To finish the design and blend the long slim tassel strands into the more heavily beaded tassel top you need to add a random fringe of 15-20 strands around the lower quarter of the decorated bead.

Attach a new 1.5m single thread to the decorated bead to emerge 5mm from the top of the tassel strands. Reduce your colour palette to mainly greens and golds. Call this seed bead assortment X.

Following fig 13 thread on 12-15X, a flower bead and 1X. Pass the needle back up the flower bead and 6X beads. Thread on 4X. Leaving aside the last X bead pass back up the other beads just added and 4X beads of the main strand to form a side branch.

fig 13

Make a second side branch perhaps with a leaf or other bead at the end. Pass the needle back up to the top of the main strand. Make a stitch through the mesh between the beads covering the surface of the beaded bead to emerge 5-8mm along.

Repeat to make a second strand with a slightly different bead count and distribution of feature beads. Make ten similar strands spaced around the lower part of the decorated bead.

Work a second set of branched strands just above the first - make these ones shorter, and with less feature beads.

To finish dot a few very short strands into the gaps above the second set of strands to blend the surface of the beaded bead decoration into the branched stranding.

Finish off all remaining thread ends neatly and securely.

You Will Need

Materials

20g of assorted size 6/0, 8/0 and 10/0 seed beads in a mixture of sand, bronze and neutral tones A
10g of size 10/0 ceylon ivory seed beads B
8g of size 10/0 silver lined crystal seed beads C
8g of size 10/0 silver lined turquoise seed beads D
8g of size 10/0 silver lined capri blue seed beads E
3g of size 3 silver lined capri blue bugle beads F
8g of size 10/0 silver lined blue seed beads G
3g of size 6/0 blue scarab seed beads H

An assortment of feature beads to include thirty 4mm ivory pearls J, ten 6mm turquoise pearls K and twenty each of 5mm gold filigree bead cups, semi-precious chips, 4mm crystal beads & pressed beads in neutral colours.

Forty assorted 4mm, 6mm and 6x8mm crystal beads in turquoise, teal and dark blue.
Ten assorted seaside theme pendants or beads

Three 8mm bronze crystal rounds L
One 12mm topaz fire polished faceted bead M
One 30mm round wooden base bead
50cm of 15mm wide gunmetal knitted tubular wire
80cm of stranded beading wire
Two silver French crimps
A reel of ash size D beading thread

Tools

A size 10 beading needle
A pair of scissors to trim the threads
A pair of flat-faced pliers to secure the crimp

The Tassel is Made in Five Stages

The base bead is covered in knitted wire.
The surface of the base bead is decorated.
The smaller decorated bead is made.
The tassel stranding.
The hanging loop.

Referring to steps 1 to 4 on page 102, cover the 30mm base bead with the tubular wire ready to begin the decoration.

12 Decorating the Base Bead - Using a selection from the A beads you need to stitch four or five undulating rows right around the base bead to divide it into manageable sections or strata (fig 14).

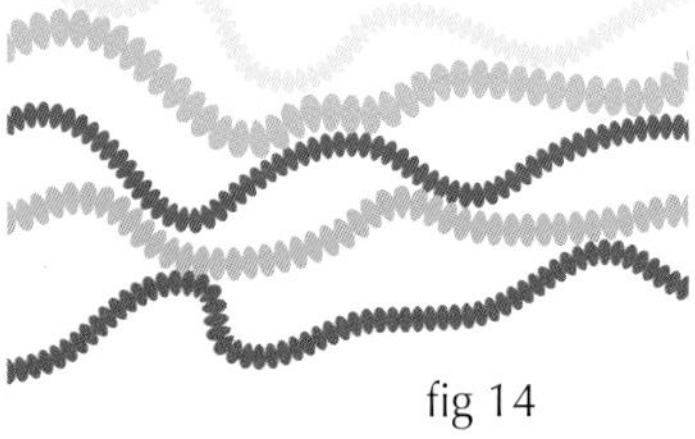

It will be easier to plan and stitch these first few rows with the larger sized seed beads (6/0 and 8/0) from your selection.

Each row is worked with one colour and size of seed bead only.

fig 14

13 Prepare the needle with 1.5m of single thread and attach it with a double stitch into the mesh at the equator of the bead. Select a colour of size 6/0 seed beads and thread on two beads.

Make a stitch that brings these two beads snug to the surface with the needle emerging two beads width further along (fig 15). Thread on two more beads.

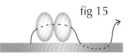

fig 15

Pass the needle back though the last bead of the previous stitch. Make a stitch through the mesh to emerge two beads length ahead of the last bead (fig 16).

fig 16

This is the back-stitch you will need to use throughout the decoration of the base bead.

When you are using smaller seed beads you will be able to thread on 3 or 4 beads at a time, if you are working a tight corner or bend you may need to secure each bead individually.

Work around the mesh to stitch a complete circuit making the undulations of various depths and widths dividing the large bead into two irregular halves. Join the last bead of the row to the first and make a single pass of the needle through all of the beads to bring them into a smooth profile.

14 Choose a seed bead for the second row. Start this row against the first row making the first few stitches run parallel to the first row. Now break away to make a new path coming back to the first row at a couple of contact points to leave interesting shapes between the rows (see fig 14). Join the two ends of the row together and finish with a pass of the needle as before.

Repeat to add two or three more rows to divide the main bead into five or six strata.

15 Examine the work. You will have lots of bends, eliptical areas and narrow spaces. Some will lend themselves to a single larger bead, some to tapered stitches of several different beads, whereas some only leave room for seed beads (see fig 17).

Stitch a few of your neutral coloured feature beads into these spaces up close to the inside of the bends to start to develop the design (fig 17).

fig 17

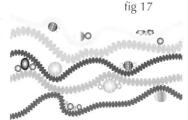

Now choose a section to work on further. Working with the same back stitch technique as before make a row of A beads to enclose the other side of the larger bead/s just added so they resemble peas in a pod. Continue with the row working right around the large base bead or bringing it back along the nearside of the adjacent main row along to create a new pocket for more feature beads. Add more feature beads if you wish.

Change to a different seed bead to make a row alongside the previous row slowly covering the section with a single layer of beads. Work until this section is covered.

Repeat this procedure all over the surface.

To complete the design you may need to stitch a few single seed beads into any gaps.

Finish off the thread neatly and securely.

16 The Small Beaded Bead - Prepare the needle with 1.2m of single thread and tie a keeper bead 15cm from the end. Thread on 1M.

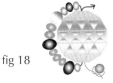

fig 18

Thread on sufficient assorted A beads to make a strap to the side of the M bead passing the needle through the large bead to pull it into place (fig 18).

Repeat the stitch with a different selection of A beads and perhaps adding a small feature bead along the length of the strap. Repeat until the M bead is completely covered with straps of beads - the straps can overlap to build up more texture if you prefer.

Finish off the thread ends securely and neaten without blocking the main hole in the M bead.

17 The Tassel - Each tassel strand grades in colour through the B, C, D, E, F and G beads to a loop of 9G just below an H bead at the bottom. The feature beads also grade in size and colour from the small pale J beads near the top through the K beads to the darkest crystals at the bottom.
The seaside themed pendants and beads add extra texture.

18 Referring to the basic tassel instructions on page 11, prepare the needle with a 2m single thread and tie 1H bead 15cm from the end with a double knot. Thread on 1L for the tassel top bead.

Starting with 8B, 1C, 3B, 2C, 1B, 4C, 1D begin to grade through the seed bead colours to make a tassel strand approximately 20cm long - do not forget to add in 5-7 similarly graded feature beads along the length.

Thread on 1H and 9G. Pass the needle back up through the H bead and all of the strand beads to emerge through the top of the L bead. Pass through the single H bead and back down through the L bead ready to make the next strand.

Make 12-14 similar strands in total in various lengths from 7cm to 19cm.

Finish off the thread ends neatly and securely.

19 The Hanging Loop - Thread the H bead at the top of the tassel into the middle of the stranded beading wire. Pass both ends of the wire up through the large decorated bead and 1L. Make sure that the L beads to either side of the decorated base bead pull up close to the hole.

Keeping the two wire thread ends together thread on three or four A beads of your choice and the small beaded bead from step 16. Thread on 2A and the final L bead. You may want to add another feature bead before you separate the wire thread ends to make the loop itself.

Thread a selection of graded seed beads, with a scattering of feature beads, as for the tassel strands onto each side of the wire.

Complete the loop by passing the two ends of the wire in opposite directions through the French crimps as in fig 9 and squash flat with the pliers to secure. Trim away the excess wire.

You Will Need

Materials

12g of size 10/0 green scarab seed beads A
5g of size 10/0 silver lined lime seed beads B
12g of size 10/0 bronzed green/purple AB seed beads C
12g of size 10/0 silver lined dark gold seed beads D
8g of size 3 green scarab bugle beads E
Fifty-five 4mm garnet AB fire polished faceted beads F
Twelve 6mm bronze crystal round beads G
Thirteen 8x6mm bronze crystal rondelle beads H
Two 8mm bronze crystal round beads J
One 15mm antique copper twisted wire flower shaped link K

Sixty assorted top drilled glass leaves in various sizes from
8x6mm to 12x8mm in toning shades of
olive green, topaz & rusty red L

One 30mm round wooden base bead
50cm of 15mm wide gunmetal knitted tubular wire
80cm of stranded beading wire
Two gold French crimps & one 4mm jump ring
A reel of brown size D beading thread

Tools

One size 10 beading needle
A pair of scissors to trim the threads
A pair of flat-faced pliers or similar to secure the crimps

The Tassel is Made in Five Stages
The base bead is covered in knitted wire.
The beaded leaves are made.
The surface of the base bead is decorated.
The tassel stranding.
The hanging loop and the small beaded bead.

Referring to steps 1 to 4 on page 102, cover the 30mm base bead with the tubular wire ready to begin the decoration.

20 The Beaded Leaves - The leaves are made from two colours of seed beads at a time - the first leaf is made from A and B beads. The method is very similar to the leaf made in the Syon Tassel chapter.

Prepare the needle with 1m of single thread and tie a keeper bead 15cm from the end. Thread on 15A.
Leaving aside the last 3A beads to anchor the strand pass the needle up through the 12th A bead (fig 19). Thread on 1A and pass the needle through the 3A beads of the anchor (fig 20).

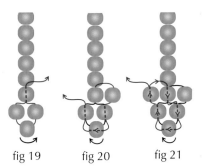

Thread on 1A. Referring to fig 21 pass the needle down through the 12th A bead, through the 3A beads of the anchor and up through the new 1A (fig 21).

fig 19   fig 20   fig 21

21 Thread on 2A and 1B. Referring to fig 22 pass the needle down through the 10th, 11th and 12th A beads of the main strand and back up the last 3A beads added (fig 22).

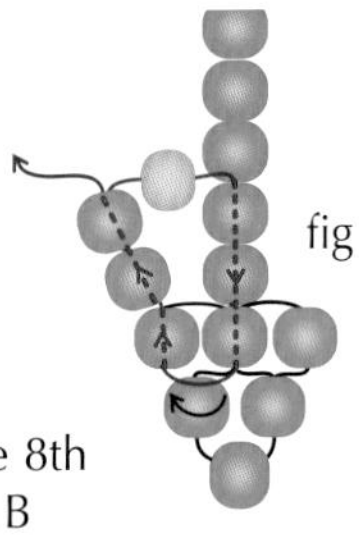

fig 22

Thread on 4A. Pass the needle down the 8th and 9th A beads of the main strand, the 1B added in the last stitch and up the first 2A of the 4A just added (fig 23).

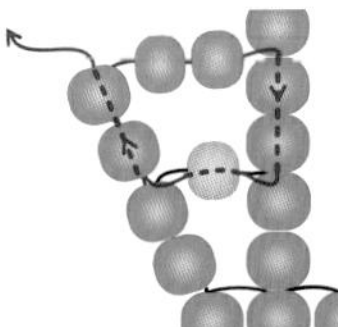

Thread on 2A and 3B. Pass the needle down the 6th and 7th D bead of the main strand, the last 2A added in the previous stitch and up the 2A from this stitch (fig 24).

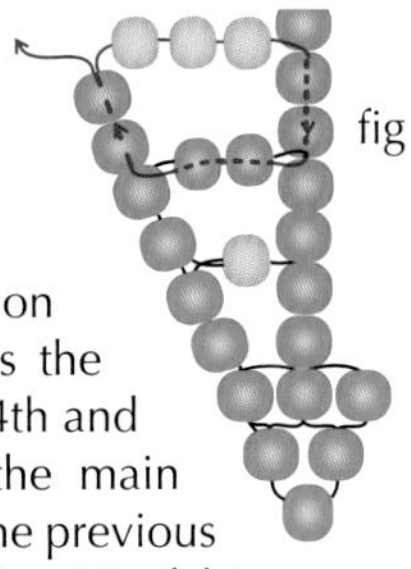

fig 23

fig 24

22 Thread on 6A. Pass the needle down the 4th and 5th A beads of the main strand, the 3B of the previous stitch and up the first 2A of this stitch (fig 25).

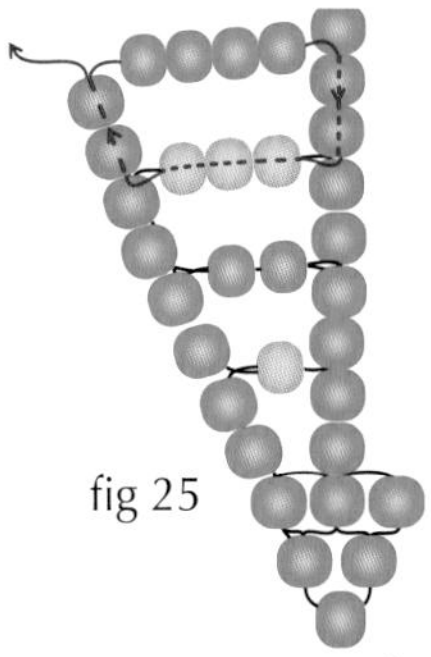

fig 25

Thread on 2A and 3B. Pass the needle down the 2nd and 3rd A bead of the main strand, the 4A from the previous stitch and the first 2A of this stitch (fig 26).

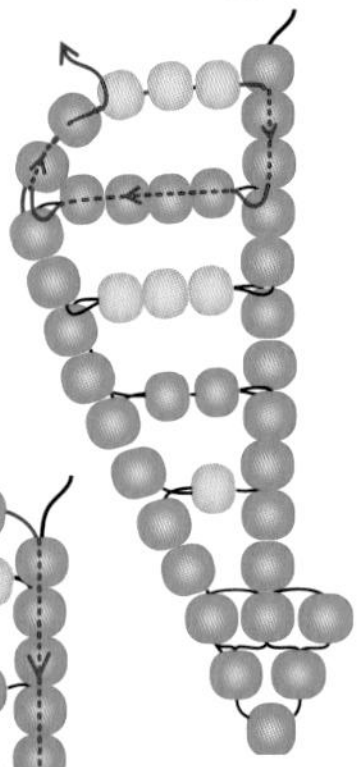

Thread on 3A. Referring to fig 27 pass the needle down the 1st A bead of the main strand and the following 11A. Pass the needle up through the top A bead on the other side of the leaf (fig 27).

Following figs 22 to 27 make a mirror image to this side of the main strand to complete the first leaf.

fig 26

Pass the needle through the A beads around the edge of the leaf to make it a little more firm. Pass the needle up through the beads of the central rib to emerge alongside the keeper bead. Remove the needle and set aside for the moment.

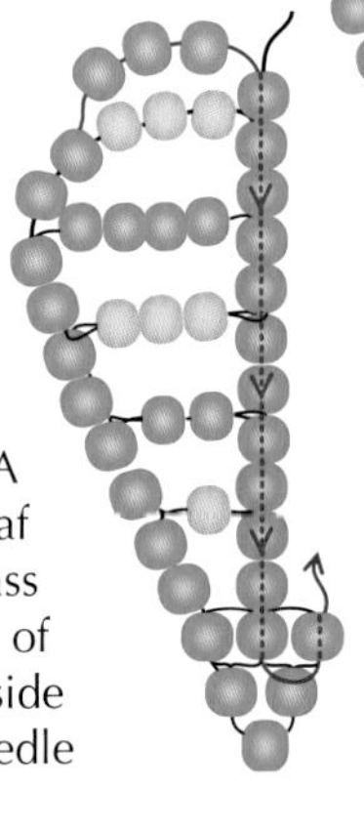

fig 27

Make three more identical leaves (four in this colourway).

Make three leaves substituting the A beads with C beads and the B beads with D beads.

Make three leaves substituting the A beads with D beads and keeping the B beads the same.

23 Decorating the Base Bead - Arrange the beaded leaves over the surface of the covered base bead to form two or three loose groupings and leaving a couple as single leaves.

Using the thread ends still attached to the leaves stitch each leaf onto the mesh through the top few beads of the central rib only, allowing the edges of the leaves to flex freely.

Attaching the beaded leaves has broken the surface of the base bead down into smaller areas. The blank areas need to be filled with a selection of L beads and several clusters of 3F. As you apply the L beads they should overlap one another slightly and tuck underneath the edges of the beaded leaves in places to give a naturalistic look.

Before you begin, put aside 11L and 24F for the tassel stranding and the hanging loop. Choose one of the bare areas and attach a new 1.2m double thread to this space, with a double stitch, approximately 6mm from the bottom hole of the base bead.

24 Thread on 1L and make a stitch through the mesh so the leaf falls into place naturally - do not pull the thread too tightly but ensure that the top of the bead touches the mesh surface.

Add a second leaf slightly higher and slightly to the left or the right (depending on the available space) up the base bead so it overlaps the first leaf by 3-4mm.

Continue to add more L beads working upwards and across the bare mesh surface filling in this area with leaf-shaped beads - try using the same L bead type in groups of three to five beads as it looks more natural than a completely random selection. Repeat around the whole base bead.

To complete the decoration add a few clusters of 3F beads into any small gaps - these will look like autumnal berries.

When the L and F beads are all applied, check to see if any beaded leaves need to be caught back to the mesh with a few stitches to make them more secure. Finish off all of the thread ends neatly and securely.

25 The Tassel Stranding - Prepare the needle with 2m of single thread and tie the 4mm jump ring 15cm from the end. Thread on 1J.

For the first strand thread on 40A, 1E, 1A, 1E, 1A, 1E, 1A, 1E, 1A, 1E, 1A, 1D, 1F, 1D, 1A, 1E, 1A, 1E, 1A, 1B, 1G, 1B, 1A, 2B, 1H, 1B, 3C, 1D, 4A, 1L and 4A.

Pass the needle back up the last D bead and thread on 3C. Pass the needle up through the last B bead (fig 28). Pass the needle through the following strand beads to emerge from the J bead at the top.

Pass the needle through the jump ring above the J bead and back down the J bead ready to make the next strand.

fig 28

Make ten further strands slightly reducing the initial A bead count each time to give a staggered set of tassel strands.

Finish off the thread ends neatly and securely.

26 The Hanging Loop and the Small Beaded Bead - Following step 16 cover 1J bead with nine or ten straps of 6C and 6D beads.

Thread the jump ring at the top of the tassel into the centre of the stranded beading wire. Pass both ends of the wire up through the decorated base bead, 1G, 1B, 1H and 1A.

Separate the wire ends and thread 9B onto each.

Thread the ends through either side of the K link and bring them together again through 1F.

Pass both ends through the small beaded bead and 1F.

Separate the wire ends and thread 1A, 1D, 1A, 1F, 1A, 1B, 1A and 1F onto each end.

Repeat until all the remaining F beads are used.

Join the two sides of the beading wire together with the French crimps (as in fig 9 on page 105).

Seasons Tassel - Winter

You Will Need

Materials

10g of size 10/0 blue scarab seed beads A
5g of size 10/0 silver lined crystal seed beads B
3g of size 8/0 frost silver lined crystal seed beads C
6g of size 3 blue scarab twisted bugle beads D
3g of size 3 silver lined crystal twisted bugle beads E
Nine 6x4mm half-argentum crystal rondelle beads F
Eleven 8x6mm blue scarab crystal rondelle beads G
Nine 8mm half argentum crystal beads H
Nine 4mm blue scarab crystal round beads J
Twenty 15mm silver snowflake pendants K
One 6x4mm blue scarab crystal rondelle bead L
One 30mm cut crystal donut
3m each of three shades of blue embroidery stranded
cotton - navy, mid-blue & grey blue
1m of blue silky rattail cord
One 30mm round wooden base bead
50cm of 15mm wide black knitted tubular wire
80cm of stranded beading wire
Two silver French crimps
A reel of navy size D beading thread

Tools

One size 10 beading needle & a size 5 crewel needle
A pair of scissors to trim the threads
A pair of flat-faced pliers or similar to secure the crimps

The Tassel is Made in Four Stages
The base bead is covered in knitted wire.
The surface of the base bead is decorated.
The tassel stranding.
The hanging loop.

Referring to steps 1 to 4 on page 102, cover the 30mm base bead with the tubular wire ready to begin the decoration.

27 Decorating the Base Bead - Prepare the crewel needle with 1.5m of the darkest blue embroidery thread. Attach the thread end to the large base bead 12mm from the top hole with a double stitch.

Using long and short stitches embroider a 20mm radiating circle about this point (fig 29). As shown leave a 2mm void in the centre or the stitches will become too bulky.

fig 29

Repeat at seven or eight more positions around the base bead to distribute the circles evenly over the surface.

Swap to the mid-blue thread and embroider long and short stitches in the gaps between the first stitches to expand the circles (fig 30).

fig 30

28 Repeat around these new larger circles with the palest blue thread. Use these stitches to merge the edge of one circle into the adjacent circle covering the remainder of the mesh (fig 31).

Finish off all of the remaining embroidery thread ends securely and neatly.

fig 31

29 Prepare the beading needle with 1m of single beading thread. If possible, trim the loop away from the top of the first snowflake pendant with a pair of sturdy scissors. Secure the beading thread and use it to attach this snowflake motif into the centre of the first stitched circle.

Repeat to attach a snowflake motif into the centre of each stitched circle.

To complete the decoration scatter-stitch a mixture of A and B beads at 3-5mm intervals all over the embroidered surface to add a little extra sparkle.

30 The Tassel Stranding - Prepare the beading needle with 2m of single beading thread and tie a C bead 15cm from the end with a double knot. Thread on 1G for the tassel top bead.

Thread on 40A, 1B, 8A, 1B, 3A, 1B, 1D, 1A, 1D, 1A, 1D, 1A, 1B, 1A, 1F, 1A, 1C, 1A, 1E, 3A, 1C, 1G, 1C, 1A, 1H, 1A, 1C, 1J, 1C, 4A, 1K and 4A.

Pass the needle back up through the last C bead and all of the following beads of the strand to emerge from the G bead at the top of the strand. Pass the needle through the C bead and back down the G bead ready to start the next tassel strand.

Make eight further strands following the same bead sequence but reducing the initial A bead count by 5A each time to give a staggered set of tassel strands.
Finish off the thread ends neatly and securely.

Combine beads, buttons, threads, ribbons and yarns to make exciting new textures and colour themes.

Summer Garden

With so many amazing buttons available nowadays, these flower shapes make a fantastic starting point for a summery flower garden theme.

Add flower beads, ladybirds and bees over a vibrant green wire-covered base bead and rose pink seed bead tassel strands for a properly pretty tassel.

Cloudy Day

Teamed with a lovely blue wire these fantastic cloud shaped buttons, butterfly beads, birds and flower motifs create a perfect cloudy sky tassel.

Add a variety of seed beads in shades of blue and opaque white for the stranding.

31 The Hanging Loop - Thread the stranded beading wire through the C bead at the top of the tassel strands.

Pass both ends of the wire up through the decorated base bead and thread on 1G, 1C and 1L. Make sure the G beads are pulled up firmly at either end of the decorated base bead.

Separate the wire ends. Thread 1 French crimp and 29A onto the first end. Pass this wire thread end through the centre of the crystal donut and back through the crimp to form a loop through the crystal donut. Pass the wire end through the following J bead and pull firmly.

Repeat with the second wire end.

Make sure the loops are the same size and the tassel is hanging vertically from the donut - if necessary adjust the 29A bead count a little. Squash the crimps to secure the loops and trim away the excess wire carefully.

Thread the blue silky rattail cord through the crystal loop to complete the design.

Night Sky

Silver wire gives a sparkly background to blue scarab seed beads and speckles of silver & gold faceted beads.

Add some sparkly dark purple crystals for planets & metallic silver for stars.

Spangle the tassels with more stars, owls and maybe a fairy too!

The gorgeous large crystal bead could be used on the hanging loop.

Index & Suppliers

All of the materials used in this book should be available in any good bead shop or online. If you are new to beading, or need more supplies, the companies listed below run fast, efficient mail order services, hold large stocks of all of the materials you will need in their stores and give good, well-informed friendly advice on aspects of beading and beading needs.

In the UK

Spellbound Bead Co
47 Tamworth Street,
Lichfield
Staffordshire
WS13 6JW
01543 417650

www.spellboundbead.co.uk

Spellbound Bead Co supplied all of the materials for the samples shown. You can buy the beads loose (wholesale and retail) or in kits (with or without instructions), for most of the designs you see here.

In USA

Fire Mountain Gems
One Fire Mountain Way
Grants Pass
OR 97526 - 2373
Tel: + 800 355 2137
www.firemountaingems.com

Shipwreck Beads
8560 Commerce Place Dr.NE
Lacey
WA 98516
Tel: + 800 950 4232
www.shipwreckbeads.com